Brian Castle has been Bish ıs been a parish priest in S n Zambia and spent a period il of Churches' Ecumenical e moving to his present position, he was Vice Principal and Director of Pastoral Studies at Ripon College Cuddesdon, Oxford. Based on his experiences in Zambia, Dr Castle has undertaken research in the communication of theology across cultures and has developed this interest in his travelling through parts of Africa, Asia and the Middle East. In addition to the publication of his research and various articles, he is the author of *Sing a New Song to the Lord* (Darton, Longman and Todd, 1994), *Unofficial God? Voices from Beyond the Walls* (SPCK, 2004) and *Reconciling One and All: God's Gift to the World* (SPCK, 2008). He is married to Jane and has three adult children and two grandchildren.

RECONCILIATION: THE JOURNEY OF A LIFETIME

Brian Castle

First published in Great Britain in 2014

Society for Promoting Christian Knowledge
36 Causton Street
London SW1P 4ST
www.spckpublishing.co.uk

British Library Cataloguing-in-Publication Data
A catalogue record for this book is available from the British Library

ISBN 978–0–281–07026–8
eBook ISBN 978–0–281–07027–5

Typeset by Graphicraft Limited, Hong Kong
First printed in Great Britain by Ashford Colour Press
Subsequently digitally printed in Great Britain

eBook by Graphicraft Limited, Hong Kong

Produced on paper from sustainable forests

To Jane, whose companionship and laughter are food for the journey, with all my love

Contents

Acknowledgements

I am grateful to so many who, knowingly and unknowingly, have helped me write this book: Dr Henry Carse, who organized some important visits for me in Israel, Palestine and Egypt as I was reflecting on this theme; the monks at St Katharine's Monastery, Sinai, Egypt, who welcomed me and allowed me to see their amazing collection of icons, which helped me focus the theme; staff at the National Memorial Arboretum for showing me the site; the community at Taizé, where part of the book was written and whose welcome and worship in their Church of Reconciliation over the years has brought alive and confirmed for me the significance of reconciliation.

Thanks also to the Revd Liz Griffiths, Dr Anne Richards, Graham and Anne Harvey, Seamus Cullen, Nikki McVeagh and my daughter Sarah Castle for commenting on some of the chapters and for providing valuable insights into the subject; also to Canon Derek Carpenter, who has not only generously given his time and wisdom as my chaplain but has gone more than the extra mile in reading the manuscript and offering his comments. In addition, he has written the liturgies, questions and prayers.

I am also grateful to Ruth McCurry at SPCK, who has been a patient and wise commissioning editor. Thanks also to bishops, clergy and laity of the dioceses of Rochester, Harare, Mpwapwa and Kondoa (Tanzania), Jerusalem and Estonia who, directly and indirectly, have provided material and insights for this book. They have been supportive and encouraging in many ways.

Finally, I want to express thanks to my wife Jane, who has researched part of the book for me, spent hours discussing it and encouraged me in its writing.

Introduction

In June 1964 Nelson Mandela was sentenced to life imprisonment for plotting and conspiring against the South African government. During the trial Mandela eloquently defended himself and his fellow-accused in a speech that admitted some of the activities of which he was accused but denied their criminality. It ended with these words:

> During my lifetime I have dedicated myself to this struggle of the African people. I have fought against white domination, and I have fought against black domination. I have cherished the ideal of a democratic and free society in which all persons live together in harmony and with equal opportunities. It is an ideal which I hope to live for and to achieve. But if needs be, it is an ideal for which I am prepared to die.[1]

Although the word 'reconciliation' was not used, Mandela's vision for freedom was, in effect, for reconciliation between black and white in a democratic society. The way he lived his life was shaped by his vision of reconciliation. Mandela's journey towards reconciliation involved conflict and struggle as well as hope and celebration. Reconciliation was not a one-off event after conflict but the journey of a lifetime. Even after he had achieved the freedom for which he had aspired, the journey still continued. At the end of his book *Long Walk to Freedom*, Mandela wrote:

> I have walked that long road to freedom. I have tried not to falter; I have made many missteps along the way. But I have discovered the secret that after climbing a great hill, one only finds that there are many more hills to climb. I have taken a moment here to rest, to steal a view of the glorious vista that surrounds me, to look back on the distance I have come. But I

> can rest only for a moment, for with freedom comes responsibilities, and I dare not linger, for my long walk is not yet ended.[2]

This brief glimpse into Nelson Mandela's journey – and I am writing this on the day of his funeral – takes us to the heart of this book. Reconciliation, for the Christian, is grasping and laying hold of that renewed relationship with God that was sealed by Jesus Christ on the cross. However, it is the journey of a lifetime whose destination will not be reached in this world. In the meantime Christians are called to shape their lives, and that of the Church and society around them, in accordance with being reconciled with God. Being reconciled with God provides the energy and impetus to be reconciled with others.

But reconciliation is not simply the preserve of Christians. God's love extends to the world, not just to a particular group of people, and to a greater or lesser extent it is possible to see God's spirit of reconciliation at work in a wide range of activities (John 3.16). I would say that if reconciliation is taking place then, acknowledged or not, the Spirit of the reconciling God will be present.

Reconciliation is understood in a variety of ways. It overflows with life, energy and contradictions. It is eagerly pursued (which will often lead to conflict), frequently claimed and rarely embraced. It is regarded as a means, goal or method – sometimes all three. It is part of the nature of God himself. Reconciliation, the desire to repair fractured relationships in order to move forward, alludes to an instinct deep in the heart of humanity.

Politicians, psychotherapists, mediators, ecologists and theologians are among the many groups who in different but related ways seek reconciliation, though each understands it differently. For the politician, reconciliation means conflict resolution; for the psychotherapist, inner healing and integration; for the mediator, enabling different parties to share a common vision; for the ecologist, finding a renewed relationship with nature and rediscovering the balance between what consumes and what sustains; for the theologian, apprehending and restoring the relationship between God and humanity. However reconciliation is understood, it cannot be pursued unless all participating in the process are willing to move to a different place. And all parties considering the need to move can generate conflict – some will think they are already in the right place, that it is others who need to move.

Reconciliation is not one-dimensional. Working towards it means exploring a number of layers and, as with an onion, when we think we have got to the centre we may be surprised to discover more. Dr Robin Eames (former Archbishop of Armagh) and Denis Bradley (former vice chairman of the police board for Northern Ireland) co-chaired the Consultative Group on the Past, whose brief was to consult across the community on how Northern Ireland society could best approach the legacy of the events of the past 40 years to help build a shared future. The violence had formally been brought to an end with the signing of the Good Friday Agreement of 1998, but more work had to be done to sustain peace. Their report was published in January 2009, and one of its observations was a need to work on ways the past is remembered so that a shared future could be built and reconciliation achieved. Reconciliation impacts on the past and the future as well as the present – each dimension needs to be taken into account.

The quest for reconciliation is shared by many disciplines, but the Christian understanding of it has a great deal to offer the wider debate on this important topic. That understanding is not simply problem-focused but involves gratitude, joy, love, hope and generosity, all of which are energy- and life-giving. Reconciliation liberates and enables – it is to be celebrated as it is being engaged. For the Christian, reconciliation is best understood and experienced through story and enabled through ritual.

It could quite rightly be said that the Church, often plagued by disputes and conflicts, would benefit from a more thorough engagement with reconciliation. Yet Jesus Christ, God's embodiment of reconciliation, attracted conflict both within the group of his followers as well as with wider society. The latter led to his death. This would suggest – and this goes against the common understanding of the concept – that reconciliation will sometimes generate conflict rather than remove it. But conflict is not always negative – it can be creative and a means of growth just as much as it can be destructive.

Reconciliation is part of God's mission – a missionary imperative for all God's followers. The Anglican Communion, through the Anglican Consultative Council (ACC), has now formally acknowledged the significance of reconciliation for mission. Since 1984 the ACC has been working on a set of characteristics of mission that can be agreed across the worldwide Anglican Communion. The outcome is the Five Marks of Mission, which have been widely accepted. Over the last few years the significance of reconciliation has been recognized to such an extent that it was formally added by the ACC meeting in November 2012 to the fourth mark of mission, which now reads: 'To seek to transform unjust structures of society, to challenge violence of every kind and to pursue peace and reconciliation.'[3]

Reconciliation is a catalyst, and one of the purposes of this book is to indicate ways that the pursuit of reconciliation can, by the way it engages with various forces, release fresh energy and open up new possibilities. Reconciliation can bring new life. It need not only be associated with the resolution of disputes but can also shape vision for the future and help define goals – it is as much about human flourishing in good times as about handling conflict in bad.

Christian theology maintains that reconciliation between God and humanity was sealed by the death of Jesus Christ on the cross. God's reconciled relationship with humanity feeds and energizes all other reconciling acts, whether between families, societies, nations or with creation. It is the task of Christians to get this message across in the communities in which they live. Reconciliation with God has already happened. However, few would dispute that there is still much reconciling to be done in our communities, societies, world and – perhaps more than anywhere else – within ourselves. Even though reconciliation between God and humanity has already taken place, Christians continue to fall out of relationship with God. But the fact that God's renewed relationship with humanity is never broken by God shows love and forgiveness without limit.

Reconciliation has already taken place, but we have not grasped it and will not fully do so in this life; which is why, though it has already taken place, we constantly need to seek it. In this book reconciliation will be referred to in this contradictory way – already a reality but also something being sought.

Among the responses to my previous book, *Reconciling One and All: God's Gift to the World*, was one from a lawyer and another from a professional mediator. The lawyer works with couples facing divorce, and the professional mediator both with companies wanting to sharpen the focus of their planning and activities and groups in dispute. Both indicated areas emerging from the book – written from a theological perspective – that were helpful in their very different areas of work, demonstrating yet again that reconciliation is a gift not just to the Church but to the whole of humanity.

This book will build on its predecessor by focusing primarily on reconciliation rather than the ingredients that make it up. To set the scene, and for those not familiar with *Reconciling One and All*, the main features from there will be rehearsed, briefly and in what I hope is a fresh and original way. The present book, like its predecessor, comes from an unashamedly Christian perspective and highlights the lessons learnt from that tradition. Chapter 1 will paint a picture of reconciliation, drawing out its significance in Christian theology. Chapter 2 will explore five subterranean streams or 'drivers' that need to be taken into account in the process of reconciliation. Chapter 3 will highlight a number of 'marks' of reconciliation – signs that may indicate that some form of reconciling is taking place. The headings in Chapters 2 and 3 are not formulated in exclusively theological language and so may speak to other disciplines. Examples within the chapters will be drawn from a variety of disciplines. Based on the arguments of Chapters 1, 2 and 3, the final three chapters attempt to map out what a reconciling life, a reconciling church and a reconciling society look like. 'Reconciling' is used rather than 'reconciled' in chapters 4, 5 and 6, as another reminder that reconciliation is the journey of a lifetime – or more.

At the end of each chapter are questions for discussion and prayers. In the Appendix are brief liturgies of reconciliation relating to the theme of each chapter. The Litany of Reconciliation from Coventry Cathedral, used by thousands of people across the world, is also there. It is of course possible to follow the thinking of the book without reference to the questions and prayers, but these are integral parts because reconciliation is not just an idea to be read about and discussed but a way of living, relating, praying and engaging. I hope readers will add their own stories and experiences to those they encounter here as a means of interacting with reconciliation.

God's reconciliation with humanity through Jesus Christ is central to the Christian faith, as it is to the theology of St Paul. This book is an attempt to see what it means for Christian life and witness to put reconciliation at the heart of who we are and what we do.

1

Reconciliation and the Christian tradition

Stories are important for reconciliation. They are a universal medium of communication, and in telling our story we are inviting listeners into our world to experience life from our perspective. In a similar way, in listening to the stories of others we are being invited into their world and given the privilege of experiencing and viewing life through their eyes. All parties can be shaped, changed, challenged and transformed by this experience if we allow it. There is an engagement with reconciliation when the story of an individual, group, people or of humanity's care for the environment dialogues with God's story.

This chapter demonstrates the centrality of reconciliation in the Bible, highlights the significance of St Paul and then shows reconciliation weaving through the lives of two figures in the Christian tradition – Antony of Egypt and Mary Slessor. Antony of Egypt, who lived in the late third and fourth centuries, is considered to be the father of Christian monasticism, and Mary Slessor, born in mid-nineteenth-century Scotland, was a missionary to West Africa. It shows people's lives being profoundly affected when coming into contact with God and God's story. Energy, life, contradictions and conflict are features in all these stories.

Reconciliation and the Bible

Genesis and Revelation, the first and last books of the Bible, frame the story of reconciliation between God and his creation.

Genesis tells the story of a creation in harmony with its creator God that then goes all wrong; Revelation ends with harmony restored.

The first frame is the third chapter of Genesis, which relates how man and woman, succumbing to the wiles of a serpent, attempted to be God, as a result of which they fell out of relationship with God, their inner selves and each other. Furthermore their action forced God out of relationship with his creation:

> The LORD said to the serpent, 'Because you have done this, cursed are you among all animals and among wild creatures; upon your belly you shall go, and dust you shall eat all the days of your life. I will put enmity between you and the woman, and between your offspring and hers; he will strike your head, and you will strike his heel.'
>
> To the woman he said, 'I will greatly increase your pangs in childbearing; in pain you shall bring forth your children, yet your desire shall be for your husband, and he shall rule over you.'
>
> And to the man he said, 'Because you have listened to the voice of your wife, and have eaten of the tree about which I commanded you, "You shall not eat of it", cursed is the ground because of you; in toil you shall eat of it all the days of your life.' (Gen. 3.14–17)

The final frame can be found in the last chapters of Revelation, which draw a picture of God at home with humanity and creation:

> 'See, the home of God is among mortals. He will dwell with them; they will be his peoples, and God himself will be with them; he will wipe every tear from their eyes. Death will be no more; mourning and crying and pain will be no more, for the first things have passed away.' (Rev. 21.3–4)

> Then the angel showed me the river of the water of life, bright as crystal, flowing from the throne of God and of the Lamb through the middle of the street of the city. On either side of the river is the tree of life with its twelve kinds of fruit, producing its fruit each month; and the leaves of the tree are for the healing of the nations. (Rev. 22.1–2)

The 64 books in between Genesis and Revelation tell the stories of God reaching out to re-establish his relationship with his people and creation. Although the word 'reconciliation' is rarely mentioned, it flows through the Bible like an underground river, quietly giving sustenance to what is happening on the surface but occasionally forcing its way up there, where it can be identified. The word 'enmity' – which was put between the serpent and humanity (Gen. 3.15) – is the very opposite of reconciliation.

God begins his work of reconciliation through Abraham (Abram), whom he calls away from his familiar, ancestral home in Haran into an unknown future. Through Abraham he plants the seed of what will become the people of Israel, whom he wishes to use to reach out to others. God tells Abraham that in doing God's work, Abraham will be a blessing to others. Then there is a string of other characters whom God calls to be part of his work of reconciliation – Jacob, Joseph, Moses, King David and Isaiah, to name but a few. Some had behaved badly in the past – Jacob was a cheat and a liar, Moses a murderer and David an adulterer. Yet God was able to use unlikely and often unsavoury people – many of whom today would be considered psychologically unsound and unappointable to church positions – in pursuit of reconciliation.

A crisis, life-changing experience or willingness to go out of their comfort zones is required of any who are willing to be part of God's work of reconciliation. Abraham left his ancestral home (Gen. 12.1); Jacob faced one trauma after another, beginning with cheating his brother Esau out of his inheritance and culminating in a wrestling with God followed by Jacob's personal reconciliation with Esau (Gen. 27—33); Joseph was beaten and left for dead by his brothers (Gen. 37); Moses had to flee for his life from Egypt after killing an Egyptian (Exod. 2.11); David, after committing adultery and having his mistress's husband killed, was condemned by the prophet Nathan for his actions and lost his son (2 Sam. 11—12); Isaiah was forewarned that his message would be falling on deaf ears (Isa. 6.9–13). Yet God was able to use such a rag-bag of characters plagued by traumatic and uncomfortable circumstances to reach out to his people to re-establish a relationship with them.

Abraham established the line in the land that was to become Israel; Jacob ensured the line continued; Joseph took God's people into safety in Egypt when their future was under threat; Moses took them back to their own land after helping them reform their identity as that people; David united a divided people around a kingship and a centre that was to become the heart of Israel; Isaiah warned them of impending disaster because they were turning away from God.

But God does not bring about the long-term reconciliation he desires so earnestly through these people. Finally he sends himself in the person of his son, Jesus Christ. In the eyes of the world this is a great failure because Jesus is killed on a cross surrounded by nobody except his grieving mother and a close friend (John 19.26–27). However, the crucifixion is a turning point not only in the story of the Christian faith but also in that of reconciliation, because the death of Jesus is an indication of God's deep commitment to the people and the world that constantly turn their back on God's advances. The crucifixion is the very point at which reconciliation between God and his people is achieved. Reconciliation involves contradiction.

God's working towards reconciliation can be clearly traced as it flows through Scripture. The word itself may not be frequently used, but that is the direction in which God is working. It is the apostle Paul who identifies reconciliation as a theme and places it at the heart of his thinking and theology.[1] To appreciate the distinctiveness of reconciliation from the perspective of Christian thinking, it is crucial to explore how this happened. So now we turn to a closer look at Paul's life and writing, showing how his personal experiences, shaken and stirred by his relationship with God, shaped his understanding. There will be resonances with some of the stories noted briefly above.

Reconciliation and St Paul

Saul was a troubled and fanatical person, probably someone with whom it was stimulating to be – for short periods. But thank God for that as it served both Judaism and, later, Christianity. He had an impeccable Jewish background that was enhanced and confirmed by his eagerness to remove those who threatened Judaism in any way (Phil. 3.4b–6). It was his fanatical elimination of followers of the 'way' (Christians) that was the turning point in his life and ministry: this was the crisis through which Saul became Paul, finally coming to the realization that reconciliation was the lens through which God was working with the world and of which Jesus Christ was the embodiment. This was a crucial moment in Paul's personal journey of inner reconciliation.

The crisis is depicted by Luke in the book of Acts (9.1–9). Saul – as he was then known – was on his way to Damascus to get permission for the arrest of any who deviated from the Jewish faith and were supporters and followers of Jesus Christ. It was on this journey that the crisis came to a head. St Luke paints this as a blinding vision in which Jesus speaks to Saul, asking why he was persecuting him. Saul came to discover that the very Jesus whom, through his followers, he was persecuting was indeed alive and the key to a living relationship with God. This experience initiated a major shift in his theological thinking. He came to realize that his relationship with God depended not on the Law but on a relationship with Jesus Christ.

A number of years passed before the Saul on his way to Damascus became the Paul who began a wide-ranging public ministry. He did not have everything sorted out in his mind by the time he reached Damascus. There were many years of soul-searching and inner conflict before he worked out the implications of his new discovery for his own belief and faith. After Paul had begun his public ministry he recognized that he was a work in progress, 'forgetting what lies behind and straining forward to what lies ahead' (Phil. 3.13). This was for him, and continues to be for those on a similar search, a lifetime's quest. Even after Paul realized that he had been reconciled to God, he needed to discover what this meant for his life and ministry. He came to see that reconciliation with God was a source of life, energy and creativity, as the life and witness of Paul and the Christian communities he fostered and founded revealed. He found that seeking this reconciliation also brought conflict and uncertainty. Paul's central concern was to inspire reconciling communities of Christ to illustrate and proclaim God's reconciliation of the world.[2]

Reconciliation with God was at the heart of Paul's rejoicing. He knew that the life, love and witness of Jesus Christ were living proofs of that reconciliation. From this flowed reconciliation with others, with oneself and with creation. Paul was a reconciled reconciler.[3] In his second letter to the Corinthians he writes of the reconciliation that has already happened between God and his Church and the task of the Church to be the instrument of reconciliation in the world:

> All this is from God, who reconciled us to himself through Christ, and has given us the ministry of reconciliation; that is, in Christ God was reconciling the world to himself, not counting their trespasses against them, and entrusting the message of reconciliation to us. (2 Cor. 5.18–19)

For Paul, flowing from reconciliation with God are the personal, social, political and cosmological aspects of life. In chapters 5—8 of his letter to the Romans, Paul is like an impressionist painter rapidly, sometimes manically, threading together experiences and images that provide a background to reconciliation. Here Paul makes it apparent that his world had been turned upside down by the realization that access to God is not through the Law but through Jesus Christ, and he recognizes that anybody taking this reality seriously will face similar upheaval in their lives. Through his personal struggles and reflections he is brought to the radical conclusion that Christ's sufferings, viewed as a mark of failure by the world, have become a source of strength and new possibility. All this is an indication of God's love for humanity. Paul is deeply aware of the frailty of human nature and the inner turmoil that goes on within everybody, particularly within himself: reconciliation involves conflict (Rom. 7.14–25). But he is utterly convinced that despite human prevarication and failure, nothing in heaven or on earth can ultimately thwart human beings from receiving the love God is offering through Jesus Christ.

If Romans 5—8 recount the thinking behind reconciliation, in chapters 12—15 Paul tells his audience what this means for daily living:

> Let love be genuine. (12.9)
> Bless those who persecute you. (12.14)
> Live in harmony with one another. (12.16)
> Owe no one anything, except to love one another; for the one who loves another has fulfilled the law. (13.8)
> Love does no wrong to a neighbour; therefore, love is the fulfilling of the law. (13.10)
> We who are strong ought to put up with the failings of the weak, and not to please ourselves. Each of us must please our neighbour for the good purpose of building up the neighbour. (15.2)

These words are concrete advice to women and men in the particular context of the Church in Rome. God's reconciling actions have definite outcomes in the way people relate to others. Chapters 12—15 are the response to the theology of chapters 5—8.

And there is more. The letter to Ephesians reminds hearers that even those who were 'far off' (2.13) – and here there is a reference to the Ephesians who were Gentiles by birth – have been brought near by what God has done in Jesus Christ.

Furthermore Creation herself is affected by this act of reconciliation. Paul hints at this in his letter to the Romans (8.19–23) and emphasizes it in that to the Colossians (1.15–23) where, in Christ, God reconciled all of creation (v. 20). In this passage Paul is quoting from a hymn sung by the people in Colossae that shows that reconciliation with God embraces the whole of creation:

> For in him [Jesus Christ] all the fullness of God was pleased to dwell, and through him God was pleased to reconcile to himself all things, whether on earth or in heaven, by making peace through the blood of his cross. (Col. 1.19–20)

Antony of Egypt

But God's work of reconciliation did not cease with the writing of the New Testament. On a Sunday morning around the year 270, in a small Egyptian village, the following words from St Matthew's Gospel were read: 'If you wish to be perfect, go, sell your possessions and give the money to the poor, and you will have treasure in heaven; then come, follow me' (Matt. 19.21). Sitting in the congregation was a young man called Antony who, on hearing these words, decided to pursue a life of poverty and solitude. Undoubtedly Antony would have been struggling with questions about the way he was being called to serve God, and this particular event may have strengthened his resolve and clarified the direction in which he was being called. Few noticed Antony's decision at this time, but his walking into the apparently uninhabitable and inhospitable desert marked the beginning of Christian monasticism, which encompasses desert spirituality. Even though few may have noticed Antony going into the desert, when he died at the grand old age of 105 the desert had become a city. Thousands had regularly come to him to be taught, and many made the desert their home. Those who did are known as the Desert Fathers and Mothers.[4]

Like so many before him, Antony of Egypt heeded the call of God, but for him it took an extreme and somewhat bizarre form. Responding to God's call required him to be part of God's work of reconciliation. To understand this it is important to reflect on the path Antony took.

Antony entered the desert at a time the Church was facing persecution, but believed the Church did not provide the right environment for his calling as a follower of Jesus Christ to develop and deepen. Accordingly he needed to find God through poverty and solitude, and the best place for him to do this was in the desert environment with which he would have been familiar from birth. This is not the path along which God calls everybody but it is the one along which God calls some, and certainly Antony. What will become apparent is that there are elements in Antony's life that are shared by all Christians, though the specific path he took is certainly not de rigueur for all Christians.

Antony's way of developing and deepening his relationship with God was by self-denial and turning his back on the world. He recognized that struggle, particularly inner struggle, was part of life, and recognizing and accepting this was an indication that he was taking the call of God seriously. The paradox of Antony's quest for solitude was that it attracted many people to the desert and to his door because they recognized the authenticity of his response to God's call – they saw him as a holy man. Antony was reconciling his own life to God's call and in this way he was drawing others to a life of reconciliation. The words already quoted from Paul's second letter to the Corinthians summarize his actions, 'God . . . has given us the ministry of reconciliation . . . in Christ God was . . . entrusting the message of reconciliation to us.' (2 Cor. 5.18–19).

Parts of the Church were facing persecution when Antony first entered the desert, but 40 years later, in 313, a new relationship started with the Church when the Emperor Constantine proclaimed himself a Christian and the Edict of Toleration was issued. The period of persecution formally came to an end. While many Christians rejoiced at a new relationship with the state, some were dismayed that this was leading the Church to compromise its witness. This was a period when many more retreated to the desert to live the life of faith they no longer felt able to live under a new, more relaxed regime. When the Empire relaxed its harsh attitude towards Christianity, Antony intensified his asceticism and withdrew into even deeper solitude. But the crowds continued to search him out.

Although we know about the life of Antony through a biography written by Athanasius, we know about his character and faith, and indeed those of many other men and women who made their homes in the desert, through the sayings collected by their followers. The sayings are pithy, down-to-earth and direct; simple, profound and wise. There is nothing mystical about them and they challenged contemporary spirituality with their radical living out of the gospel. One of the points that frequently comes across is that our relationship with God is bound up with our relationship with our neighbour. The sayings are uncompromising in asserting that our relationship with eternal truth and love does not happen unless we mend our relations with those around us. A saying of Antony sums this up: 'Our life and our death is with our neighbour. If we gain our brother, we have gained God, but if we scandalise our brother, we have sinned against Christ.'[5]

The sayings are at heart about reconciliation, both within us and between people. They encourage their listeners to grasp the reconciliation that has been brought through Jesus Christ in the way they treat their neighbour. Many sayings from the Desert Fathers and Mothers would be at home in modern manuals on reconciliation.

The bridge between the ascetic Antony of Egypt and a contemporary example of a person continuing the reconciling work of God is provided by another saying attributed to Antony. Antony was revered as a very holy man and this particular saying would speak into that context. It also challenges a modern-day assumption that only the 'professionals' – that is, monks and nuns – can begin to aspire to the fullness of relationship with God that Antony had reached:

> It was revealed to Abba Anthony in his desert that there was one who was his equal in the city. He was a doctor by profession and whatever he had beyond his needs he gave to the poor, and every day he sang the Sanctus with the angels.[6]

Mary Slessor

Life was tough and food was scarce for those living below the poverty line in the industrial cities in nineteenth-century Britain. Mary Slessor, the second of eight children, was born into a working-class family in Aberdeen in 1848, though she spent most of her early days in Dundee. Her father, when sober, was a shoemaker – her devout, praying mother needed to bring up and fend for her children. After the family moved to Dundee (in the vain hope Mr Slessor would lay aside his drinking and start afresh), she worked half-time at a factory and attended its school for six hours after work. When she reached the age of 14 Mary worked full-time and attended evening school. Mary's hero was the missionary and explorer David Livingstone and, like her hero, she would work at the loom with a book propped up, snatching moments to read amid the noise of the machinery.

Mary's life was spread between work in the factory, education and attending the local church, where her leadership capacity was utilized. Her courage and character were apparent when she confronted hostile gangs of boys on the way to church and persuaded them to attend with her. It was in 1875 – two years after Livingstone's death – that she followed his call to be a missionary and went to Calabar, West Africa, known as 'the white-man's grave' because of the climate and conditions. Mary spent the next 40 years there, moving deeper into the remote forest regions. Like Antony of Egypt, Mary Slessor took the risk of moving into the remote and unfamiliar where she felt more at home and in pursuit of an inner reconciliation.

She quickly became fluent in the local language, took a broad view of local beliefs and customs and saw in the people a belief in God, though she was concerned about their fear of evil spirits. A non-judgemental attitude and deep care and concern for people endeared her to those with whom she worked and to whom she ministered. Not surprisingly her commitment to the welfare of the people was recognized more widely. She was enrolled as an Honorary Associate of the Grand Priory of the Hospital of the Order of Jerusalem, and when she died in 1915 was buried in the land she loved with the equivalent of a state funeral.

Mary Slessor was known for a number of achievements but three are of particular significance for reconciliation.

First, she was called on to settle disputes, which she did in a variety of ways. One of her most dramatic interventions, which shows her courage and character, was the occasion she ran ahead of two groups of warriors about to go into battle with each other. She stood between the two spear-carrying groups and argued with the chiefs until they agreed to give up their feud.

Second, she rescued unwanted children. There was a belief among some tribes that twins came from evil spirits and when twins were born, they and – sometimes – their mother were killed. Wherever she could, Mary Slessor rescued the twins and brought them up in her own home. On occasion, before it was discovered that twins had been born, she would smuggle one of the twins away, hidden in a pot, so that mother and one child would survive and be accepted in the community.

Finally, she had a particular concern for women's welfare. Women were poorly treated. Mary looked after their needs whenever she could and established the Slessor Industrial Home for Women and Girls, where there was training in crafts and trades that would help in life and survival.

Mary Slessor's story provides insights into reconciliation at a number of levels. There is no account of a call as dramatic as that of St Paul or St Antony, but her response was no less radical, being willing to go to different and unfamiliar places. Such a willingness would have helped Mary grasp more deeply God's act of reconciliation in Jesus Christ towards her. The outcome was witnessing to reconciliation in the communities she founded and in which she worked. Her own life had been transformed by her experience of God and God's story and, in turn, she transformed people and communities. Energy, life and creativity are signs of the transformation. In her settling of disputes, concern for unwanted children and the founding of the Industrial Home for Women and Girls, she was an agent of reconciliation and she formed communities of reconciliation.

Some contemporary reflections

Over the last 20 years the significance of reconciliation in theology and in practice has been recognized. Whereas reconciliation has been acknowledged as part of Paul's theology, it has not until recently been a high-profile area of study. The increased appeals for reconciliation in national and international arenas in the resolution of disputes have prompted theologians to look afresh at this concept that is central to Paul's theology. While many view reconciliation as the heart of the gospel, some would go further and say that reconciliation *is* the gospel.[7]

Another indication of the prominence of reconciliation is that it has been put firmly on the agenda of the Church of England by the Archbishop of Canterbury, Justin Welby, who has denoted reconciliation as one of his ministerial priorities and has appointed an adviser in reconciliation to his staff.

The reason for giving such examples from the Christian tradition is to focus on the significance of reconciliation in the Christian story. Each community and each person is called by God not to imitate those who have gone before but to learn from and be inspired by them as we try to discern the distinctive path along which God is calling us in our own reconciliation and in our calling as agents of reconciliation.

Some lessons about reconciliation from the Christian tradition

While the word 'reconciliation' does not appear many times in Scripture, the concept of reconciliation is the thread that gives coherence and momentum to God's relationship with the whole of creation. God's love compels him never to give up on the world. The genius of St Paul is that he identifies and develops the theological significance of reconciliation, providing a lens through which one can view and interpret God's engagement through scripture and beyond. Jesus Christ is the embodiment of reconciliation, and the cross is the gateway to reconciliation. Furthermore engaging in reconciliation is not simply an activity required of Christians but is part of the nature of God. Understanding God as Father, Son and Holy Spirit points to the nature of God, who is continually engaged in reconciliation within himself. Those who respond to the call of God – and this chapter has given some examples – are called to be part of his reconciling work. As each apprehends what it means to be reconciled with God through Jesus Christ, so too has each, in the words of St Paul, been given the ministry of reconciliation and entrusted with the message of reconciliation.

Here are some reflections about reconciliation gleaned from the examples in this chapter. Some will be expanded in later chapters.

1 Humanity fell out of relationship with God, each other and creation. God, through those whom he has called, has sought to reconcile these relationships. God has brought about reconciliation through Jesus Christ. Reconciliation, then, is a gift of God.

2 Reconciliation is not one-dimensional but relates to all parts of life. It is about the relationship between God and humanity, between human beings, between nations, between communities, between humanity and creation and finally, and perhaps most pivotally, the relationship a person has within his- or herself.
3 It is a requirement of all parties involved in reconciliation – especially those who consider themselves in the right or the innocent party – to make a journey, usually outside their comfort zone.
4 The desert experience is important in reconciliation. This is not surprising as it is an ever-present reality in Judeo-Christian history and is regarded in theology as a place of reviewing – sometimes offloading – the past, renewing and forming a new identity. While it may not be necessary to go to the desert in pursuit of reconciliation, it is necessary to go through the desert experience.
5 Forgiveness is an essential element in reconciliation.
6 Recognition of and respect for the 'other' is another essential element of reconciliation. The 'other' in Scripture is the neighbour, the stranger, the foreigner, the orphan, the widow, the outcast and the poor. The Jewish and Christian faiths require their followers to have a special care and concern for these people. Behind this lies an understanding of the 'otherness' of God, and Christians would say that Christ himself is present in those regarded as 'other' by the world.
7 Apart from St Paul, the figures in this chapter may not have been aware that they were involved in reconciliation. They were attempting to walk in the direction that God was calling them, and when they did this they were automatically making God's gift of reconciliation a reality in their various contexts. This had an effect not only on the particular situations they were addressing but also on what was going on within themselves.

8 It is possible to distinguish between reconciliation as God's gift and reconciliation as a human imposition. Reconciliation that can help all the parties involved grow and flourish, even though getting there may involve conflict, is a gift of God. Reconciliation that, through the pretence of peaceful negotiation, sacralizes a previous injustice, usually of the stronger party over the weaker party, is not God-given and is storing up disaster for the future. This could more properly be termed 'conflict resolution' rather than reconciliation. Reconciliation can only happen between parties who regard themselves as having equal say and status in the negotiation.
9 Reconcilers attract those seeking reconciliation and, through their example, send out others to undertake reconciliation. The most obvious example is St Paul who, in response to his encounter with Jesus Christ on the road to Damascus, set out to found and establish many churches, communities of reconciliation. In the desert, Antony attracted people seeking personal reconciliation, and as a result of his influence a number set up other desert communities.

For individual, quiet reflection

1 The chapter contains many examples of people God has used for the purpose of reconciliation. Reflect on those with whom you can identify and the reasons you identify with them.
2 How can you apply St Paul's injunctions in Romans 12.9–21 to your own life and relationships? What are the marks of love being 'genuine'?
3 Think of somebody with whom you would like to be reconciled. Is there anything that prevents you from taking the first step?

For discussion in groups

1 What stories, in the Bible, of reconciliation between God and his people are the most memorable and meaningful? Why are they meaningful?

2 Does a person sometimes need to be reconciled with parts of him- or herself? In what way?
3 What use is a desert experience in our lives today?
4 Who is the 'other' in our world?
5 Can reconciliation happen when both sides do not have an equal share in the negotiation?

Prayer

Father God,
you stand with those who are hungry in a world of plenty;
with those who thirst for springs of water;
with those whose nakedness shames not them, but us;
with the stranger seeking friends;
with the sick whose inner healing only you can bring;
with those in prison who long to hear the voice of freedom:
give us the gifts of generosity, love and compassion,
that standing with You and serving them we may witness to
your saving grace
in Jesus' name. Amen.

Derek Carpenter

2

Drivers of reconciliation

If reconciliation in all its fullness is being sought, then it is essential to take into account memory, forgiveness, victimhood, otherness and gift. These five are subterranean streams or drivers – similar to the propellers of a ship – that give momentum and provide coherence to groups or individuals in their seeking of reconciliation. Memory and remembering are powerful factors in shaping our identity. Forgiveness provides a radical way of relating to others and to ourselves. Victimhood determines whether a person or a group are the subjects or objects of their context. Otherness makes it possible to be fed and challenged by what lies beyond, and it allows God into the process. Gift is a reminder that nobody has a monopoly on reconciliation but that it comes, sometimes unexpectedly, from God.

Memory and remembering

The Anglican Cathedral in Grahamstown, in the Eastern Cape of South Africa, tells the history of the area through the monuments on its walls. A significant part of that history was dominated by the Xhosa Wars (1779–1879) fought between the original residents of the land and the European settlers, and a number of the monuments to fallen soldiers refer to the opposition in the battles using racist language that is no longer acceptable in the Rainbow Nation of South Africa. This became a particular problem in post-apartheid South Africa – black South Africans found it difficult to worship in a building where their ancestors were referred to in such derogatory terms. The church authorities were faced with a dilemma: should they remove the memorials that were commentaries on significant parts of South African history or should the memorials remain, causing offence to many who worship in the cathedral? There were staunch protagonists for both positions. In 1995 a plaque was erected trying to put the issue in some perspective, the following words from which contain the dilemma:

> There is a wide variety of memorial tablets and plaques in the cathedral. Not all of them are written in language that would be used today. Some words on them are offensive to us all. They are not conducive to affirming the relationships which lie at the heart of the Christian faith and to which this building and its community witness . . . for the moment the plaques remain as part of our common history, and as a sign of our need for penitence. They exist alongside the signs of our duty to be grateful for the acts of courage and faith of the past as well.

However, at the same time students training for ministry at the College of the Transfiguration in Grahamstown were reluctant to worship in the building because of the wording on some of the plaques and, after lively discussion, the offensive words were covered with marble strips, known locally as 'marble Tipp-Ex™'.

This example from Grahamstown indicates that it is not only memories that are significant in shaping our identities but the way one remembers. The European settlers may have interpreted their struggle as being against an 'inferior' people, but those whom the settlers displaced remember the loss of their lands and the approach of Colonel Graham – after whom their town was named – to displace the local Xhosa residents 'With a proper degree of terror'.[1] Both groups viewed and related to the same event in different ways – the way they remembered kept them apart.

The way they viewed the situation depended on how they considered they were treated at the time and also their current position in relation to those historic events. The descendants of the displaced local residents harboured a sense of injustice that they could not publicly voice during the apartheid years. But now, as they regained the dignity of local residents once more, they could articulate their outrage and object to the way the story of their past was being told by others through the wording of the memorials. In order to move forward, and certainly for the different communities to move forward together, two changes were necessary. First, they could no longer regard each other as strangers but needed to trust each other as friends. Second, they needed to work on the way the past was to be remembered and, ideally, agree a shared commentary on it. Each community needed to learn new stories about one another and themselves.

The current website of Grahamstown Cathedral describes the memorial plaques that have focused so much discontent and then reports: 'The emphasis now is on reconciliation.' That single sentence written in the context of the memorials is a powerful reminder that memory and the way we remember are crucial factors in moving along the path of reconciliation.

In the heart of England, not far from Lichfield, is the National Memorial Arboretum (NMA). Set in 150 acres of woodland, the arboretum is the UK's Centre of Remembrance and it exemplifies a different way of remembering. Opened in 2001, it hosts memorials to a range of organizations including military, civil services (police, ambulance, fire and rescue), charities and other organizations, both at home and overseas. At the heart of the site is the Armed Forces Memorial that lists the names of all those who have died in service since the end of the Second World War – around 16,000 women and men. There are two sculptures that, in a very moving way, bear silent witness to the cost of armed sacrifice. One depicts a mother and child holding each other and an elderly couple clutching each other in grief, weeping over their husband, father and son whose body is being carried by his comrades. The other depicts a woman and some Ghurkha soldiers preparing a fallen warrior for burial – a figure before double doors points to a world beyond where the warrior will rest, as another figure chisels the name on the memorial.

The alignment and axis of the memorial are significant. Drawing inspiration from prehistoric monuments, on the eleventh hour of the eleventh day of the eleventh month, Remembrance Day, the sun's rays stream through the door of this sculpture, illuminating the wreath in the centre of the memorial.

'Shot at Dawn' is a particularly moving memorial in the arboretum. A stone sculpture of tied and blindfolded 17-year-old Private Herbert Burden stands in front of 306 stakes – the number shot for cowardice and desertion in the First World War. Six trees stand to attention in front of Private Burden representing the firing squad. 'Shot at Dawn' is deliberately located in the most easterly point of the arboretum so that it is the first part of the site to be lit up by the morning sun. Eventually 17-year-olds were not allowed to fight on the front line, but this was brought into effect after the execution of Private Burden of the Northumberland Fusiliers and Private Herbert Morris of the British West Indies Regiment. In 2006 all those shot for desertion in the First World War received a posthumous pardon.

There is nothing triumphalist about the way the NMA remembers those who have lost their lives in the service of the country. One group is not regarded as inferior or superior to the other. War is not glorified, but regardless of whether it can be justified, its cruelty, injustices and sheer inhumanity are themes playing not far below the surface. The NMA 'remembers' war as a place where heroes are to be found but not as a place of glory, for if it were such a place, that would be a justification of all the killing. Above all the arboretum is a place where the nation thanks families for giving their loved ones in the service of their country.

What is distinctive about the arboretum is the way of remembering. There is something deep in the human psyche that requires every person and every nation to honour the memories of their departed loved ones and fellow citizens. This is the reason memorials are erected and flowers are laid at places where death has occurred, whether by war or by accident. The NMA remembers in a spirit of humility and thanksgiving: while remembering the departed it is expressing the nation's gratitude to their families. It is not scapegoating and demonizing an enemy, placing on them all the blame for the death and destruction – this way of remembering will lead to further conflict as people seek to avenge their dead. The NMA's way of remembering recognizes that all parties need to share some of the responsibility for the failures that led to war, so the focus is not on the enemy or even the victory over the enemy but on a thanksgiving for the departed. Such ways of remembering enable people to move forward towards reconciliation.

The Canadian philosopher and former politician Michael Ignatieff takes this thinking a step further. He argues that revenge is a ritual form of a community's respecting and remembering of their dead. If citizens are killed in conflict there is a primal urge to honour their memories and sacrifice and justify the cause for which they died. This is revenge. Urges for revenge can lie sleeping beneath the surface for many generations before they eventually flare up, but flare up they will. Breaking the cycle of revenge and working for reconciliation will only begin when communities once at war with each other can learn to remember and mourn their dead together.[2] Both Grahamstown Cathedral and the NMA seek to remember in ways that do not store up potential problems for the future.

Memory and remembering are powerful factors in shaping identity. The way memories are used – the way we remember – is key to reconciliation. It is possible to remember an event in a way that will lock us in the past by making us want to avenge wrongs of the past. Alternatively it is possible to remember in such a way that the past event does not imprison us in the past but liberates us in order to move forward.

Victimhood

The early 1970s saw the beginning of an economic 'miracle' in South Korea. After a long period of harsh occupation under Japanese forces, the Korean peninsula was the object of a deal between the USSR, USA and UK. Within a few years the cold war, which was being played out in the region, spilled over into the Korean War in 1950. That war added even greater misery to the Korean people. Seoul, the capital, had changed hands four times and had been flattened; millions of people were left homeless; industry had been destroyed; the countryside had been devastated; the economy was in a mess. It was out of this that the economic miracle of the 1970s quickly brought South Korea acknowledgement as a power that needed to be recognized and taken seriously by leading world economies.

However, South Korea's new-found economic prominence was achieved on the backs of the poor. While a large number of people became wealthy, a larger group of ordinary people – known as the *minjung* – were experiencing harsher conditions. The *minjung* provided the labour for Korean industry to grow but they themselves were growing poorer and being maltreated by a repressive government and unreasonable employers. It was in these conditions that, in the late 1970s and 1980s, 'Minjung theology' emerged. Minjung theology articulated the Christian faith using Korean symbols and ways of thinking because the traditional western articulation of the gospel could not reach deep down into Korean souls. It was formulated from the perspective of the *minjung*, the poor and marginalized in Korean society. As Minjung theology was making its mark, resulting in the arrest and harassment by government of its proponents, Minjung churches and Anglican sharing houses appeared. In these the love of God and liberating power of Jesus Christ were being shown in practical ways, such as offering food, encouraging the *minjung* to set up their own working cooperatives and helping them resist oppression in their daily lives from such issues as extortionate rents. Minjung theology came to be regarded as a theological resistance movement.

One of the key messages the theology promoted was that people should not be regarded as the objects of their history, rather as the subjects. Indeed one of the key writings in the area is *Minjung Theology: People as the Subjects of History.*[3] If the *minjung* are the objects (which is the way they were regarded), then they are being 'done unto' – they have no say or control over their lives. Whereas if they are the subjects, then their worth is acknowledged – they have a say over their lives and the way they are treated. To put it in a different way, Minjung theology was arguing that the people should not be treated as victims by others; nor should they accept victimhood, because it prevented them from growing into the people God had created them to be.

Victimhood is the enemy both of reconciliation and of a healthy faith. Minjung theology's assertion that the people should resist victimhood reflects the message of the Christian gospel. Nevertheless over the centuries the Church has encouraged people to take on the mantle of the victim because, some would say, Jesus Christ was a victim. It is certainly true that the Jewish sacrificial system is used by some New Testament writers to explain Jesus' self-giving at Calvary, but to go on from there and regard victimhood as a virtue because Jesus was a victim is to misread and misinterpret the text. Sadly the Church has done this for many centuries.[4] Jesus Christ was never a victim as victimhood is understood today – he does not fill that role in the way the twenty-first century understands victimhood, which is as a person or a people permanently powerless in the face of the violence of others. At some point we may all be victimized; that does not make us victims. We may not have a choice about being victimized; we do as adults have a choice about allowing ourselves to become victims. St John's Gospel makes Jesus' relationship to victimhood clear:

> And I lay down my life for the sheep . . . For this reason the Father loves me, because I lay down my life in order to take it up again. No one takes it from me, but I lay it down of my own accord. I have power to lay it down, and I have power to take it up again. (John 10.15–18)

Nelson Mandela was imprisoned by the apartheid regime in South Africa. The authorities had him in prison, had control over his whereabouts, but they did not have control of the man. This was powerfully illustrated when they offered to release him provided he agreed to conditions about what he could and could not say on his release. Mandela refused. Eventually they agreed with Mandela and even the President of the Republic had to visit him while still in prison, before Mandela finally agreed to be released.[5] Mandela may have been victimized by the authorities, but he was no victim. The irony is that while in prison he never lost his authority, and towards the end of his time there had more power than those wanting to release him.

Another example of somebody refusing to accept victimhood is the nineteenth-century American hymn-writer Fanny Crosby, whose most famous hymn is 'To God be the glory'. In its last verse are the words, 'But purer, and higher, and greater will be/Our wonder our transport when Jesus we *see*.' The 'see' is particularly significant because Crosby, who wrote thousands of hymns, was blind from the age of six months. Life was a struggle for her but she refused to become a victim of her circumstances. She wrote about her blindness in this way:

> It seemed intended by the blessed providence of God that I should be blind all my life, and I thank him for the dispensation. If perfect earthly sight were offered me tomorrow I would not accept it. I might not have sung hymns to the praise of God if I had been distracted by the beautiful and interesting things about me.[6]

In order for Fanny Crosby to be on the path of inner reconciliation – and her hymns chart her own journey towards God – she needed to reject victimhood. Life appeared to have inflicted a cruel blow on her and, like the resurrected Jesus Christ, she would always have to carry the wounds. But like Jesus Christ himself, her wounds were transformed and became a means for the creation of hymns from which many have benefitted. Furthermore Crosby regarded her disability as a means for achieving something she would not have achieved had she not lost her sight.

Another powerful example of people refusing to accept victimhood was seen in the inspirational Paralympic Games in 2012 in the UK. Athletes suffering from horrendous disabilities were able to perform to athletic heights of which the majority of 'able bodied' people could only dream. One cannot underestimate the struggle that many paralympians have had to face, but their achievements are indications that they have turned their backs on victimhood.

Victimhood bars the route to reconciliation of any kind. Being a victim means being trapped in the circumstances that have been victimizing, and that is not a state in which our humanity – both personal and corporate – will flourish. One of the marks and geniuses of being human is an ability to draw on the spiritual aspect of our personality in order to rise above what is holding us back. If the process of reconciliation is to be taken seriously, there can be no victims.

Yet in some parts of twenty-first-century Britain, victimhood is encouraged and viewed as a virtue. A popular media ploy is to encourage people who have suffered terrible losses or maltreatment to give emotional interviews in order to say how their lives have been permanently damaged by what has happened. It is important not to underestimate another's suffering and trauma, but for the media to give this so much prominence is not only intrusive and prurient but also encourages society in its victimhood mentality. It reinforces the victim's sense of being trapped. A refusal to move out of victimhood brings societal paralysis and keeps people as the objects of their history, preventing them from being the subjects.

The director of a conflict-resolution centre working with Palestinians and Israelis commented that he sees two countries – Palestine and Israel – vying to be regarded as victims because this justifies the attitude and actions the one takes against the other. Again the path towards reconciliation is slowed and even halted, and victimhood is playing a role in the conflict.

In summary, victimhood makes a person or a people the object of their story whereas they need to be the subjects if they are to grow and flourish. People may have no choice about being victimized but they have a choice about remaining victims. Nelson Mandela, Fanny Crosby and athletes in the Paralympic Games are examples of people who refused to accept victimhood. There is a significant strand within twenty-first-century British society that encourages victimhood, viewing it as similar to a virtue. Such encouragement will trap people in their victim status and prevent growth. Reconciliation is not possible while there is a victim. Jesus Christ was never a victim in the way that victimhood is understood today.

Forgiveness

Just as reconciliation cannot take place if victimhood is present, neither can it if forgiveness is absent. While it is possible to have forgiveness without reconciliation it is impossible to have reconciliation without forgiveness. Christianity has developed an understanding of forgiveness found nowhere else, and its radical nature has the capacity to transform both Church and society. Forgiveness means that a relationship can continue regardless of any wrong perpetrated. The relationship after the wrong committed and forgiven may not be the same as it was before (it may even be stronger), but as a result of forgiveness it will continue.

The social theorist Hannah Arendt writes that Jesus Christ was the first to discover the significance of forgiveness in the realm of human affairs. The fact that this discovery was made by a religious figure in the context of a religious ministry and is articulated in religious language does not preclude its use in a more secular context.[7] The Church does not find the radical nature of forgiveness easy. Society as a whole, struggling with a low view of humanity, fed and encouraged by an overinfluential media, finds it impossible to forgive. Yet there are heroic exceptions.

The film *Les Misérables*, released in January 2013, is about forgiveness. In an early scene Jean Valjean, a convict on parole, is given hospitality by the Bishop of Digne. While he is with the bishop, Valjean is caught stealing two silver candlesticks. The Godly bishop, instead of allowing the police to arrest Valjean, forgives him. Valjean is so deeply moved that he sets out on a journey that transforms him from a criminal filled with hatred for humanity to a self-giving hero ready to go the extra mile for those in real need. The film is based on Victor Hugo's book of the same name and, in turn, leans heavily on the very popular stage play, where the religious themes of forgiveness and redemption are drawn out. In an Easter sermon a previous Archbishop of Canterbury, commenting on the scene in which Bishop Digne forgives Valjean, said that it contained the finest description of grace outside the New Testament.[8]

On Christmas Eve 2012 a church organist was on his way to play for the Midnight Mass in his church in Sheffield. Before he reached the church, 68-year-old Alan Greaves was brutally attacked. He died three days later from his horrendous injuries – nearly every bone in his face had been broken. After two men were convicted of his murder in July 2013, Mr Greaves' widow, Maureen, said that she had no feelings of hate and unforgiveness towards her husband's murderers. In the eulogy at her husband's funeral she said:

> It has to be a daily act of saying 'I place them in your hands, God', so that I don't have to worry about them, I don't have to hate them. After the massive shock and heartbreak, this was probably the most difficult thing I have ever had to do, to go down the path of forgiving them.

> It has been a wonderful release that I have not had the burden of hatred towards them. I have to do it every day so I don't lapse. It is not an easy journey to look two men in the face who have killed the person you love most in the world and hang on to that.
>
> When you are sitting there in court and you see them and you are heartbroken at what they have done to you, they have taken from you the person who is still your soulmate, it is very difficult to sit there and continue to forgive them and want to forgive them.
>
> One thing I have comforted myself with is that the God I believe in had a son who was beaten as Alan was beaten. The God I believe in had a son who was resurrected as I believe Alan will be resurrected to be with God.

These frankly mind-blowing examples of forgiveness highlight one of the major challenges of the New Testament, namely the requirement on every Christian to show, when wronged, God's forgiveness towards the one who has committed the wrong. Such forgiveness will have a profound effect on the perpetrator and also on the person wronged. The Bishop of Digne's forgiveness of Valjean shows forgiveness transforming the life of the criminal. Maureen Greaves' forgiveness of her husband's killers shows that forgiveness brings liberation to the one who has been wronged because failure to forgive and carrying the 'burden of hatred' will imprison the one wronged in the past. The forgiveness shown by both the Bishop of Digne and Maureen Greaves indicates that both know what it means to be forgiven and loved by God.

In the Lord's Prayer we pray that God may forgive our sins as we forgive those who sin against us. This is the nature of God's forgiveness towards us, and we are called to forgive others in similar kind. Once we have turned to God, saying sorry for what we have done wrong is not to persuade God to forgive us but to open ourselves to receive his love and forgiveness. Even though God forgives, there may be issues of justice that need to be addressed, especially if another is harmed, but this does not detract from the radical nature of forgiveness, which has its source in God and which the followers of Christ are enjoined to reflect. This is the point at which our commitment to reconciliation is truly tested. The consequences of not forgiving are strained relationships with God, each other and ourselves. Not forgiving is also a block to reconciliation.

Musalaha – named from the Arabic word for reconciliation – is an organization set up to work on reconciliation between Israeli and Arab Christians. When Arab and Israeli Christians meet together they share a faith in Jesus Christ but their social and political backgrounds often divide them. This division became very apparent at an annual women's conference whose theme was forgiveness. Israeli women there were asking forgiveness for Israeli aggression against Palestinians but were disappointed that Palestinian women were not reciprocating for Palestinian aggression against Israelis. At the same time Palestinian women thought that the severity of the situation they faced was not being understood or believed by the Israeli women. It is not uncommon in such situations for one side to underestimate the difficulty and suffering faced by the other – seeing them for what they are would require a major shift both in thinking and in action, and such shifts can be costly. This was certainly the experience of the Jerusalem Center for Jewish–Christian Relations (JCJCR).

Located in West Jerusalem, the JCJCR has the task of establishing dialogue between Christians and Jews, taking particular account of the significance of religion. A dialogue was established between some Jews and Armenian Christians. The Jews spoke about the Holocaust and persecutions faced by European Jews, the Armenians about the dreadful persecutions they had faced over the years. The Jews were amazed to hear that the Armenians too had faced persecution and ethnic cleansing. An experience of the JCJCR is that one side does not want to hear of the other's trials and tribulations because it would force perpetrators to look afresh at their own experience of persecution in the light of their persecution of the other. Accordingly Israelis did not want to hear of the persecution of their enemies and if they did, were reluctant to recognize its full impact. Similarly Palestinians, in the light of their own current sufferings, were reluctant to hear about the Holocaust. It is difficult to ask for forgiveness if one party does not accept the damage being done to the other. If forgiveness is to work, openness and honesty are required as well as a willingness to change one's thinking and attitude.

Forgiveness has its roots in the Christian faith. Forgiveness provides a radical way of relating, enabling a relationship to continue after a wrong has been committed. It can bring transformation to the person who commits the wrong and liberation to the one who forgives. The consequences of not forgiving are strained relationships with God, each other and ourselves. Not forgiving is a block to reconciliation. Seeking forgiveness requires an honest and realistic awareness of the harm done to the other, and recognizing the extent of that harm requires a willingness to change, both in the relationship and in the way we think about the other.

Otherness

The word 'otherizing' is gaining momentum in the USA. It describes placing people outside the circle of 'us', which often means regarding or treating them as threats or even enemies. The extreme of otherizing someone is viewing them as inferior and subhuman. One consequence of otherizing is an accumulation of fear – fear *towards* the other that in turn builds up fear *within* the other. When the other person is regarded as a threat, other ideas, attitudes and customs are viewed in a similar way.

While the tendency to recognize the other as a threat accurately reflects an understanding all too prevalent in much of society today, it goes against the understanding of the other in both Jewish and Christian traditions. In Scripture the other is always personalized: the neighbour, the stranger, the foreigner, the orphan, the widow, the outcast and the poor are the equivalents of the other. Hence the people of Israel are required to take particular care of this group of people because they were once in their position, and accordingly have their roots in them. This is drawn out every harvest when the people make their offering and are required to make this response: 'A wandering Aramean was my ancestor; he went down to Egypt and lived there as an alien, few in number, and there he became a great nation, mighty and populous' (Deut. 26.5).

The very identity of the people of Israel depended on their care of those others on the edge of society because the Israelites themselves had been on the edge. The prophets were quick to remind the Israelites of this whenever they neglected or mistreated the poor and strangers, threatening them with dire consequences (Amos 5.21–24; Mal. 3.5). This concern for the other marked out Israel from its neighbours.

Jesus Christ further radicalizes the concern for the other. Scattered throughout the New Testament are indications that he turned his back on power, lived on the edge of society and had a special concern for those whom others rejected – focused and crowned by the fact that he died the death of an outcast and criminal (Phil. 2.6–8; Matt. 2.13–15; John 8.2–11; Luke 23.32–33). Jesus' radicalization of concern for the other is seen in his call not simply to reach out to those on the edge but to love our enemies: 'You have heard that it was said, "You shall love your neighbour and hate your enemy." But I say to you, Love your enemies and pray for those who persecute you' (Matt. 5.43–44).

And even more strongly:

> But I say to you that listen, Love your enemies, do good to those who hate you, bless those who persecute you, pray for those who abuse you. If anyone strikes you on the cheek, offer the other also; and from anyone who takes away your coat do not withhold even your shirt. (Luke 6.27–29)

The most powerful embracing of the other comes when Jesus is dying on the cross and says, 'Father, forgive them; for they know not what they are doing' (Luke 23.34).

It is important to emphasize that the concern for the other is not only the ethical consequence of the Judeo-Christian tradition but is at the heart of its theology because it points to something important about God. In the Hebrew Scriptures awe, holiness and fear are terms used in reference to God. Theologically this is described as 'transcendence'. Another word that embraces these terms is 'otherness'. God is wholly other. In Jesus Christ, God takes on the vulnerability of being human and, with his friends and followers, walks the paths of Palestine. God is at the same time both wholly other from and fully intimate with humanity. Otherness and community are bound together in the Christian understanding of God.

Relating to the other is key to the process of reconciliation – it is not by accident that one of the components of the Greek word for reconciliation used in the New Testament means 'other'. It is necessary neither to like nor agree with the other but it is important to respect and even welcome them – hard as it may be – in the process of reconciliation. However, the most challenging part is the embracing of the enemy who may have persecuted, struck, abused, stolen from and even tried to kill us – and even actually killed others close to us.

Of all that is required for reconciliation, reaching out and embracing the other is one of the most challenging in western society. Western culture has established the custom of trying to import itself into different corners of the world – such as Iraq, Afghanistan, parts of Africa – where the other is regarded as the enemy or inferior and, as a consequence, fear becomes dominant. Fear of the other is becoming more prevalent in the UK: while it is important to be sensible about security, there is a strong undercurrent, fuelled yet again by a hysterical media, that heightens concern about the other. There is fear about other cultures, ideas and attitudes. If a society is fearful of the other then it cannot articulate and own a vision for itself.

Relating to the other is central to the identity of the Jewish and Christian faiths. Judaism requires its followers to reach out to the neighbour, the stranger and the poor whereas Christianity radicalizes this demand by requiring its followers to love their enemy and those who do them harm. Such an approach is totally alien to western culture, where 'otherizing' symbolizes relationships with those around. Otherizing views those outside the circle of 'us' as threats or enemies. Relating to the other is key to reconciliation – is it possible for it to take place in any context in a culture where otherizing is part of the fabric of society?

Gift

Reconciliation is a gift of God and, as we have already observed, Christians are called to minister this gift on God's behalf (2 Cor. 5.18–19; see Chapter 1, p. 12). Reconciliation is embodied in the life and person of Jesus Christ who is God's gift to the world, and if we are to begin to apprehend the gift of reconciliation, let alone minister it on God's behalf, it can only be through a deepening relationship with Jesus Christ. Thus reconciliation is more than a process, as mediation and conflict resolution are processes, but it is a whole way of living, providing a framework within which we order our lives and relationships with God, each other, ourselves, society and creation. Reconciliation can also shape vision and define goals. It releases fresh energy and opens up new possibilities. Just as Jesus Christ is the embodiment of reconciliation, so, for the followers of Jesus, reconciliation is central to their identity.

Too often reconciliation is regarded simply as sorting out relationship problems – between people and nations – so that they can live together without harming each other. Many would regard mediation and conflict resolution as reconciliation, with the removal of conflict and the outbreak of peace as a sign that people are on the way to achieving reconciliation. There is more to it than that. One of the tasks of the Christian Church and Christian theology – that is, all those to whom the ministry of reconciliation is entrusted – is to ensure that reconciliation in all its fullness is made available to the whole of God's creation. Reconciliation is part of God's mission, which makes it a missionary imperative of all God's people.

Enjoying the fruits of reconciliation is not limited to the followers of Jesus Christ but is available to all. Reconciliation is indeed God's gift to the world and not simply to Christians. Society at large has recognized that the Christian faith has a significant contribution to play in reconciliation through the leading roles played by Christian leaders such as Archbishops Desmond Tutu in South Africa and Robin Eames in Northern Ireland.

Recognizing reconciliation as a gift means that no one party has possession – and therefore control – of it. All parties need to look beyond themselves for it and, together, agree when it becomes part of their relationship. Like birdwatchers in the spring eagerly awaiting the return of a rare bird after its winter migration, it needs one person to see it coming and other members of the party to confirm its identity. Such mutual recognition sets the tone for the framework in which reconciliation needs to be sought. All parties need to regard themselves as equal partners, a relationship of interdependence needs to develop and there needs to be a quiet patience.

Finally, it is customary in most cultures to recognize, in a gift, the generosity and love of the giver and to receive it with gratitude and joy. Generosity, love, gratitude and joy do not naturally spring to mind when reflecting on processes of reconciliation. Yet while recognizing that there will be struggle, distress and conflict in reconciliation, where are the signs of the resurrection that enabled the marks of death on Jesus' hands, feet and side be to be seen as the proof that he had been raised? Where is the joy, generosity and love that open up the ways to new, deeper relationships? These would be real signs that reconciliation is regarded as gift, even God's gift.

Reconciliation is God's gift to the world and not simply to Christians, whose task it is to be ministers of reconciliation. Recognizing and treating reconciliation as God's gift is difficult. Yet recognizing it as a gift affects the tone and atmosphere in which it takes place and will enable the relationship between the parties involved in reconciliation to develop. The presence of joy, generosity and love are indications that reconciliation is recognized as gift.

For individual, quiet reflection

1 Reflect on times when being reconciled has released fresh energy and opened up new possibilities.
2 Who are the 'others' in your everyday experience for whom you need to have a special care and concern? Are there those – in family, workplace, community or church – whom you find it easier to ignore or forget? How can you change this?
3 Have you experienced a grudging acceptance of an apology or have you been reluctant to offer forgiveness? What do you think have been the motives behind gifts you have been offered. What has motivated your own giving to others?

For discussion in groups

1 If you have visited it, share your experiences of the National Memorial Arboretum and its effect on you. In the light of the statuary already there, what work of art would you devise as a sculptor or an artist to bring the past into the present, as remembrance does, and to point to a more hopeful future?
2 Discuss a film or play – perhaps *Les Misérables* – that has a message about forgiveness. Does it contain a helpful portrayal of forgiveness?
3 Who are the 'victims' in today's society – and is it in their control or only in that of others to reverse their role?

4 What can the Church do, formally and informally, to promote reconciliation, so that openness can be encouraged, forgiveness offered and lives made whole?

Prayer

God of love, whose Son stretched his arms upon the Cross to embrace a fallen world,
we pray for healing where there is brokenness:
for peace where there is conflict and disorder;
for harmony where wholeness needs to be restored;
for forgiveness where we have strayed from the path of love;
and for reconciliation where relationships have been severed.
This we ask in the name of your Son, whose death brought life and whose resurrection brings the gift of life eternal and the promise of a kingdom
where peace, harmony and forgiveness reign
and all are reconciled in you,
Father, Son and Holy Spirit. Amen.

Derek Carpenter

3

Marks of reconciliation

For over 2,000 years the Church has grappled with reconciliation and has some insights to bring to the topic. Having explored the drivers of reconciliation in Chapter 2, this chapter draws together some threads to create a living tapestry illustrating the distinctive insights and questions the Christian tradition brings to this important topic. These are the marks of reconciliation. While the elucidation of each section draws on Christian theology, the headings could speak to everybody wanting to pursue reconciliation.

This is not a 'manual for reconciliation', nor is it a 'how to do reconciliation' chapter, nor does it pretend Christianity has a monopoly on reconciliation, though God needs to be present for it to be reconciliation. By both drawing and building on previous chapters and my earlier book,[1] this chapter highlights some questions that need to be asked and issues that need to be taken into account.

In addition it is important to remember that reconciliation is not primarily problem-focused – nor is it simply a technique to be used by specialists for mediation and conflict resolution. Reconciliation is the concern not just of every Christian but of every human being. The aim of this chapter, and indeed the book, is to journey towards a fuller, more integrated and more holistic understanding of reconciliation, and in pursuit of this it offers 15 'marks' of reconciliation. It is not an exhaustive list and they do not all have to be present as an indication that a journeying towards reconciliation is taking place. However, if none are present the question needs to be asked whether it is reconciliation that is being pursued. The remaining chapters 'test out' these marks and questions on some contemporary situations.

Fifteen marks of reconciliation

Reconciliation is a lifetime's quest and journey

Reconciliation is not an isolated, one-off event, rather it is a way of life, shaping our attitudes and providing a way to articulate our beliefs. Once it is accepted that God has already reconciled the world through Jesus Christ, the primary task of Christians is to point to that reconciliation, focus it and help make it a reality in the communities in which they live and work – which will include families, church and world – and within themselves. All of this will involve a change of culture that will place reconciliation at the heart of the gospel, where conflict will be regarded as full of potential and opportunities, dialogue and relationship are seen as essential to healthy living and we learn to live with conflicting truths rather than think we need to choose one over the other.

Reconciliation is not the same as mediation or conflict resolution, though these terms are frequently used synonymously. Mediation and conflict resolution can be paths to reconciliation. While there will be occasions when disputes are resolved, long-sought-after agreements reached and self-discoveries made, these are small victories (reconciliations with a small 'r') on the way to Reconciliation (big 'R'), which is a full and complete realization that we are embraced by the infinite love that is God. This is the answering of the prayer in the letter to the Ephesians that:

> you may have the power to comprehend, with all the saints, what is the breadth and length and height and depth, and to know the love of Christ that surpasses knowledge, so that you may be filled with all the fullness of God. (Eph. 3.18–19)[2]

Such complete Reconciliation with God (big 'R') will be experienced not in this world but in the next. Nevertheless, the small victories (reconciliations with a small 'r') are glimpses, experiences and foretastes of the fullness of what is to come.

But the quest and journey towards reconciliation is not only a Christian pursuit. Many faiths encourage their devotees to seek a relationship with the deity they worship and with their neighbours. People of no faith recognize the need for human beings to work at their relationship with their communities and even with the planet. There are many movements, both religious and non-religious, that encourage people to strive for an inner harmony and integration. And there is a recognition that the way individuals relate within themselves has an effect on the way they relate to others outside of themselves and even to the planet. The search for reconciliation is hardwired into humanity, and Christianity has this at the heart of its theology. The challenge for Christians is to witness to this priority and remind society of its importance.

Reconciliation flourishes and deepens in a climate of celebration and thanksgiving

Reconciliation is fuelled by celebration and thanksgiving. Although problems and difficulties will be faced and encountered and injustice and suffering may be involved, reconciliation is not primarily about problems. In fact reconciliation will not be possible in an environment that is primarily problem-focused. To embark upon reconciliation, all parties must be willing and eager to take this step and all must regard themselves as equal partners in the process – there can be no coercion.

Reconciliation cannot take place while the battle is raging, only after all involved have reached the point where the desire for peace is greater than that for war. Finding the right moment to embark upon reconciliation in a dispute is crucial, and creating the right atmosphere for the process is vital. A climate of celebration and thanksgiving is eschatological in that one can begin to enjoy now something that can be fully enjoyed in the future – reconciliation will in the end be achieved because it has already been achieved, and such assurance gives momentum to the process.

Reconciliation is a source of new energy, life and hope

One way of knowing whether one is pursuing reconciliation is that it releases new energy, renews life and kindles fresh hope among all involved. Amid all his struggles, St Paul discovered a new vision for his life, for the Christian faith and redefined the meaning of hope. The National Memorial Arboretum is providing the nation with a new way of remembering that does not depend on the glorification of war or demonizing of the enemy.

Reconcilers establish reconciling communities

Reconciliation also brings life and hope in that those seeking reconciliation for themselves and for others beget and encourage reconciling communities. St Antony of Egypt was on a personal journey of reconciliation that resulted in his drawing many to him seeking his wisdom, and the formation of communities in the desert that were also seeking reconciliation. Mary Slessor was on a similar journey. She was recognized as a reconciler and sought to bring reconciliation in a variety of disputes. St Paul, constantly in pursuit of reconciliation as he was defining it, founded Christian communities that, amid their conflicts, were communities of reconciliation. The seriousness with which reconciliation is taken by a person or group will be reflected by their encouragement and growing of other communities of reconciliation.

Relationship is a cornerstone of reconciliation

Jesus Christ is the embodiment of reconciliation: Christians are being constantly called into a deeper and fuller relationship with Jesus Christ and therefore with reconciliation. A key insight of the followers of St Antony – the Desert Fathers and Mothers – is that relationship with God is inextricably entwined with relationship with neighbour. It is impossible to love God and at the same time show hatred towards one's neighbour.

But when there is dispute and disagreement there will always be a tendency to 'otherize' or objectify the opposing party. First there may be a playful belittling of the other's views ('How can anybody possibly think like that?'), then a belittling of the person themselves ('What a fool/idiot/troublemaker'). Belittling can then turn to demonizing and regarding the other as less than human ('animal/terrorist/heretic' or worse). When a person is put into the category of being less than human, that provides the justification to treat that person in less than human ways. Belittling gestures can culminate in genocide. Beneath one exhibit in Yad Vashem, Israel's Holocaust Memorial Museum in Jerusalem, is a quotation from the German Jewish poet Heinrich Heine, who around 1820 wrote in his play *Almansor*: 'Where they burn books, they will also ultimately burn people.' Heine's books were among those burnt in 1933 in Nazi Germany.

Dick Sheppard was a well-known and much-loved Vicar of St Martins-in-the-Fields, London, in the 1920s. When asked whether he loved a certain difficult and demanding member of the congregation, Sheppard replied, 'I do more than love him, I even like him.' Loving a person recognizes him or her as a human being created and loved by God. Loving does not necessarily mean liking or even agreeing, but it does mean respecting the humanity of the 'other' and regarding that person as a subject rather than an object of any encounter. Forming a relationship with the person, persons or even part of oneself with whom one wishes to reconcile makes it more likely that one would view the other as a fellow human being. Relating in this way to an enemy as well as a neighbour is essential to reconciliation.

In May 2013 the Commonwealth Secretariat convened a high-level round-table meeting on post-conflict reconciliation. Commonwealth countries that have been involved in post-conflict reconciliation were invited to share their reflections on processes for handling these experiences so that others could build on them as a basis for post-conflict reflection and nation building. In the gathering, Lord Allerdyce, a former Speaker of the Northern Ireland Assembly, said that experience had shown that when people feel valued, respected and given dignity they are more likely to be receptive to dialogue. This is another reminder of the importance of relationship.

Finally, without the relationship brought about by dialogue, the very first steps towards reconciliation cannot be made. It was only after there was dialogue between opposing sides in Northern Ireland that it was possible to inch towards the Good Friday Agreement of 1998. It will only be after dialogue with the Taliban that there will be any hope of a peaceful settlement in Afghanistan. It is only when a person is willing to have that inner dialogue with her or his conflicting desires, passions and beliefs that there is the possibility of journeying towards an integrated and fulfilled life. Dialogue does not mean agreement, but it does mean relationship.

Reconciliation draws all involved into the 'desert'

All people involved in reconciliation are drawn out of the familiar into a new land. This may be a geographical move, as it was for St Antony and Mary Slessor, but is just as likely to be a change of attitude, understanding or belief in which the world is seen differently – that was St Paul's experience. Such a change will necessarily mean spending some time in the 'desert', which is a period of disorientation, uncertainty and fear, en route to a new place. The desert need not be a physical place – it could well be an inner experience that reflects the apparent barrenness of the desert. Those who know the desert well say that it is not without life but one needs to know where to search for it. The Church Fathers and Mothers came to realize that they did not have to go *to* the desert to find God, they had to go *through* it.

Rowan Williams views the harshness of the desert positively as a pathway to God and not as a trial of spiritual strength:

> The desert means a stepping back from the great system of collusive fantasy in which I try to decide who I am, sometimes to persuade you to tell me who I am (in accord of course with my preferences), sometimes to use God as a reinforcement for my picture of myself and so on and on. The 'burden' of self-accusation, the suspicion of what the heart prompts, this is not about an inhuman austerity or self-hatred but about the need for us all to be coaxed into honesty by the confidence that God can forgive and heal.[3]

It is not just one party that needs to be open to change in the process of reconciliation. In God's working with humanity he initially tried to bring about reconciliation with Abraham and the prophets. When this did not work he had to become involved with the world in a different way in the person of Jesus Christ. All need to be open to change.

The willingness of the parties involved in reconciliation to spend time in the desert is an indicator of their commitment to reconciliation – it is only when a person is fully committed to the journey that reconciliation is possible.

Reconciliation requires listening

Listening to the story of another, especially if the other is regarded as an enemy, is extremely difficult because it may undermine the position of the listener. Bassam Aramin is a Palestinian member of Combatants for Peace, an organization of former Palestinian and Israeli fighters who are working for peace in Israel–Palestine. Bassam, whose ten-year-old daughter was killed by a plastic bullet, described the first time he saw a film about the Holocaust, which helped him begin to understand what the Jewish people had experienced:

> One of the problems with our communities is that we are shielded from ever seeing things from the point of view of the other side. I knew nothing about the Holocaust. I couldn't believe what I was watching. It explained so much about the Jewish people, to see what they had gone through.[4]

In Bassam's case his community had 'shielded' him from the reality of the Holocaust, but as the previous chapter showed, the experience of the Jerusalem Center for Jewish–Christian Relations went further. They encountered in some instances a reluctance for groups to accept the impact of the persecution or suffering that another group had encountered; to do otherwise would require a reassessment of their own suffering in the light of the suffering of the enemy.

Listening is so difficult because there is a temptation to evaluate what is heard and formulate a response before the speaker has finished. While this is true in every part of life, it is particularly significant when during reconciliation somebody speaks with honesty and integrity about something very intimate. From a faith perspective it is important to remember that if someone cannot provide the inner space to listen to another in conversation, then that someone would not be available to listen to God in prayer.

The importance of storytelling and narrative in reconciliation

Just as listening is an important part of reconciliation, so too is storytelling. Storytelling is a non-elitist activity – you do not need an education to tell your story. Storytelling is very personal – you cannot disengage yourself from your story. Storytelling includes in the narrative the emotions, the perspective and the world view of the narrator. Storytelling is something that has no age limit. Storytelling has no cultural barriers – even if we have no knowledge of a particular culture, we learn a lot by listening to stories about it. Storytelling is a universal medium of communication capable of reaching deep into our souls, more so than anything else – apart, perhaps, from song.

But there is another important dynamic when people tell their stories. Stephen Grosz, an experienced psychoanalyst, regards his task as encouraging people to tell him their stories because doing so helps them make sense of their lives.[5] He also maintains that if a person is not able to tell their story, the story will somehow possess the person, who may act in uncontrollable, irrational ways: 'When we cannot find a way of telling our story, our story tells us – we dream these stories, we develop symptoms, or we find ourselves acting in ways we don't understand.'[6]

Grosz's insight from psychoanalysis can be applied to other disciplines that seek reconciliation. The more fully and deeply a people, or parties, are able to tell their stories and the more fully and deeply those stories are heard and engaged with, the greater possibility there is for reconciliation. What cannot be told and what is not heard have the potential of derailing a reconciliation process and making any agreements reached superficial and short-lived.

Stephen Grosz also makes the point that all sorrows can be borne if a person tells a story about them. Those involved in pastoral work will be aware of the importance of listening to people's stories.

It was very apparent from the story about the memorial plaques in Grahamstown Cathedral that different stories can be told about the same event. The original inhabitants of Grahamstown viewed the coming of the European settlers one way, the settlers themselves another (see Chapter 2). Opposing sides in any conflict will have different stories to tell about the same conflict. A person seeking therapeutic help will need help to put in words his or her own story. As Grosz points out, if we cannot tell our story it may be expressed in different, often violent, ways.

One of the tasks in reconciliation is to put one story beside another, see where they merge and, ultimately, agree a shared story of the events around which reconciliation is being sought. In Christian worship there is a unifying of God's story with the story of humanity, and all worshippers are encouraged to bring their stories to the table. At the heart of the Eucharist the great prayer known as the Eucharistic Prayer tells the story of God's love towards creation.[7] Worshippers are reminded that even though God's people turned away from him, he constantly reached out to them, ultimately reconciling himself with humanity in Jesus Christ. Everyone receiving the bread and wine is stepping into the same drama, wanting God's reconciliation to become more real in their lives and consequently in the world.

The significance of storytelling and narrative is recognized in mediation, which can be a path to reconciliation. There are a number of models of mediation, each with different emphases and some more suitable in some contexts than others. For example, the role of mediation in the workplace is to find solutions by addressing the underlying concerns of those in dispute. This is a form of conflict resolution and an interest-based model of reconciliation is frequently adopted in such cases. But other models would be better employed in community and church mediation.[8] A more recent model is narrative mediation, a child of narrative family therapy developed in the mid 1980s. In narrative mediation people will tell their conflict stories, often casting themselves in the role of victim and protagonist over and against the party – the 'other' – with whom they are in dispute and whom they will regard as victimizers and antagonists. The role of the mediator is to challenge such stereotypes and open up stories to different interpretations and new possibilities.

Narrative mediation fits well with Christian theology which, at its best, tells the story of God's involvement with creation. It challenges the problem-solving orientation that can so easily dominate processes of mediation and indeed of reconciliation, whereby one party regards the other as the problem.

Narrative mediation also challenges the myth of neutrality, namely that it is possible for mediators to stand apart from their own contexts – social, historical and cultural – in their work. It is right that a mediator should be objective in his or her work and judgements, but objectivity is different from objectivism. Objectivism is the false belief that it is possible to be totally neutral. Nobody is a blank sheet of paper in any context, and a mediator will be affected, probably unconsciously, by a whole range of factors ranging from the emotional to the political. Every mediator will, at some level, bring an own agenda to the task, even if the task is to manage the process. Objectivity, on the other hand, recognizes that one cannot be totally neutral but that, through wisdom and experience, one can be as neutral as possible. Objectivity recognizes that mediators are not blank sheets of paper but will need at times to exercise their own judgement. The quality of a mediator comes to be recognized through the wisdom of that judgement. It is important that they be trained and wise people but also that they have a sound knowledge of the area in which they mediate. The general practice in western cultures is that mediation is undertaken by people outside the area of dispute, quite often by professional mediators. In the Middle East a wise, known and respected member of the family or community would be called upon to mediate.

Furthermore in narrative mediation there are times when mediators are required to challenge oppressive attitudes (in particular of the 'dominant' party), thereby laying aside their 'neutrality'.

Reconciliation involves conflict

Reconciliation is often linked with the removal of conflict, but this goes against the understanding of reconciliation in Christian theology. Indeed a sign that one is on the path to reconciliation is an increase in conflict. The ministry of Jesus Christ, God's embodiment of reconciliation, was marked by conflict that increased during the course of his ministry. St Luke's Gospel in particular highlights the symbolism of Jesus' journey from Galilee – regarded with disdain at the time – to the heart of the Jewish faith in Jerusalem, where the opposition to Jesus is at its strongest. The conflict reaches its agonizing height with Jesus' death on the cross, and it is at this point that reconciliation between God and humanity is achieved. When Jesus meets with his disciples after the resurrection, the wounds of the crucifixion, the marks of the conflict, remain on his body but have been transformed from the marks of death to signs of new life. Reconciliation is not about the removal of conflict, rather the transformation of conflict from something destructive to something life-giving.

Human beings face potential conflict on a daily basis, but it is only when there is negativity within it that it emerges as full-blown conflict. Two people may be deciding where to go on holiday, both with their own ideas. When the pros and cons of each place have been discussed, agreement would usually emerge. This is a potential conflict scenario, but because both parties want the same outcome – that is, to go on holiday together – there is usually mutual accommodation leading to amicable agreement. However, if there is an argument about where to go and one person accuses the other of being selfish and lacking consideration, this would lead to full-blown conflict. Conflict does not have to be confrontational but it is the context in which it takes place and the hopes, expectations and demands that surround it that will render it positive or negative, life-giving or life-denying. While 'negative' conflict can be destructive, paradoxically it has great potential for growth in the way it forces people to delve more deeply to discover a way forward. When conflict is negative and people become tired of conflict, realizing that there is more to be lost than gained from it, there comes a point when those involved recognize that change is inevitable, though it may be at great cost and after much anguish.

Conflict is essential for growth and healthy living. It is not a sign of failure or sinfulness. Indeed avoiding conflict can be a way of preventing the work of the Holy Spirit. The Church of England is facing a number of issues at present that are generating a great deal of conflict, namely the ordination of women to the episcopate, responding to the issue of same-sex marriage and the key question of its relationship with the wider Anglican Communion (some of these issues will be examined in Chapter 5). There has never been a time when the Church has not faced major issues of conflict and there never will be. What is vital is the way the issues are handled – as far as the Church's witness to the world is concerned, the way the issues are handled is as important and sometimes even more important than the issues themselves. The Church of Scotland theologian Elizabeth Templeton highlighted this as a speaker at the 1988 Lambeth Conference when the issue of the ordination of women to the priesthood was being debated. She reflected on the debate in this way:

> The world is used to unity of all sorts, to the unity of solidarity in campaigns, unity in resistance, communities of party, creed, interest. But it is not used to such possibilities as this: that, for example, those who find the exclusion of women from the priesthood an intolerable apartheid and those who find the inclusion a violation of God's will should enter upon one another's suffering. Somewhere in there, authority lies.[9]

Reconciliation is costly, painful and requires self-giving

There is no way around this, no anaesthetic that will help. Those walking the path to reconciliation will find that it is at times costly and painful and will require self-giving – being willing to give up something precious, which may be an attitude, idea, possessions or even life itself. Everybody involved in a process of reconciliation, regardless of how aggrieved they may have been, face similar challenges. The story of God's deep desire to bring about reconciliation between God and humanity did not work when he sent representatives such as Abraham, Isaac and Jacob, nor did it work when he sent Moses and the prophets. It only worked when, at great cost, God himself came in the person of Jesus Christ and was willing to give his very self for the humanity he loves so much. The cost of reconciliation was the pain, degradation and humiliation of the cross. People walking in the footsteps of Jesus over the centuries have paid a similar price. Although this may be a lonely path to take, many are strengthened and encouraged by their relationship with Jesus

Christ and by the company of others, to be found in churches and beyond, who may be walking similar paths or supporting them as they walk theirs. At the heart of the apartheid regime in South Africa, Desmond Tutu became a symbol of reconciliation as he resisted and spoke out against the evils of the regime. Archbishop Tutu's relationship with Jesus Christ and the support of his fellow Christians, both in South Africa and across the world, fed his courage and drive. It was his witness through these times that made him the obvious person to chair South Africa's Truth and Reconciliation Commission.

Not everybody walking the path of reconciliation pays the extreme cost Jesus Christ and others of his followers were called on to pay. Certainly not everybody will be working in such a high-profile way as Desmond Tutu. But for all on this particular path it will at times be costly, painful and require self-giving. Coventry Cathedral has a distinctive, worldwide ministry of reconciliation that started with the bombing of Coventry and the Cathedral in 1940. Walking in the smouldering ruins of the medieval cathedral, the Provost picked up three nails and shaped them into a cross. Since this time the cross of nails has been the symbol of Coventry's ministry of reconciliation. For Jesus Christ, wounds, nails and the cross have been marks of reconciliation. This remains the case.

Reconciliation requires transformation

If a person or group does not believe their position should change, it will not be possible to move along the pathway towards reconciliation. Reconciliation requires the transformation of all parties seeking reconciliation – it is not just the party who has inflicted hurt that needs to be open to transformation but also those who have been hurt. In order that such transformation can take place the former will have to respect the other and the latter will have to shun victimhood.

If the planet is to survive there needs to be a transformation of human behaviour. A relationship of respect and reverence will need to replace the tendency to treat the earth as a commodity.

Transformation is central to the Christian faith. St Paul was transformed from a persecutor of Jesus Christ into a follower. Death was transformed from the end of life into a new beginning. Bread and wine is transformed at the Eucharist into the body and blood of Christ. Transformation and change are key elements in reconciliation.

Reconciliation involves living with contradictions

Pursuing reconciliation requires us to live with unresolved contradictions, often two contradictory truths. Living with the unresolved can be uncomfortable and unsettling, with the result that there is always the temptation to iron out differences to make life easier. Unity becomes more important than truth.

Living with contradictory truths lies at the heart of the Christian faith, frequently posing uncomfortable questions to society's understanding of reality. The crucifixion and resurrection of Jesus Christ show that death is the gateway to life. If this is true it raises huge questions about the value and longevity society places on wealth, possessions and self-fulfilment. Again, if death is the gateway to life then there are the contradictory truths that it is a time both of grief and sorrow and of hope and joy. St Antony of Egypt, through the way that he lived, challenged contemporary wisdom by showing that life and wisdom came though denial and self-negation – the thousands who both sought and followed him came to the desert in pursuit of this contradiction. In the early centuries of the Church there were intense debates about whether Jesus Christ was God, human or God and human. If both God and human, how was this possible and was one trait more dominant than the other? Different groupings within the Church took different positions, and the debate provoked fierce and bitter conflict. The Church finally came to the view that Jesus was fully God and fully human, requiring people to hold two apparently contradictory truths at the same time. But this is not an easy position to hold. There are some oriental churches that do not accept the validity of the conferences that came to this decision. Many world faiths would argue that it is not possible for Jesus Christ to be both God and human – for many it is a stumbling block to becoming a Christian.

Currently the Anglican Church is struggling to hold together those who believe it is God's will to ordain women to be priests and bishops and those who cannot see how such a move can be justified.

The easiest way to handle the contradiction of two truths is to give one priority over the other, but the story of reconciliation teaches us to hold on to the contradiction until a larger canvas appears on which they may be reconciled. This canvas may appear tomorrow or it may not appear in this life at all.

In 1926 the composer Arnold Schönberg coined the term 'emancipating dissonance'.[10] In his music Schönberg employed atonality through musical chords that sounded dissonant to the contemporary ear and, emotionally, cried out for resolution into a sound that was pleasing and acceptable. He observed that as the ear became accustomed to the atonal sound within a particular context, the discordant atonality will eventually become emancipated from that context, find a new context and become acceptable. This has happened in music across the centuries in that musical sequences at one time regarded as atonal and discordant were heard and received without question at a later time. Other composers, including Duke Ellington, connected Schönberg's concept with society and humanity.[11] Emancipating dissonance provides a helpful way of viewing the contradictions that will be encountered in reconciliation. It is not the task of reconciliation to resolve the contradictions but to emancipate them when the time is ripe. The American poet William Carlos Williams expresses this succinctly:

Dissonance
(if you are interested)
Leads to discovery.[12]

Reconciliation and hope

The director of a conflict-resolution centre in Bethlehem was speaking about the difficulties faced by Palestinians who were being hemmed in by the separation wall surrounding the town, by the bypass roads around Palestinian territory that Palestinians could not use and by the building of Jewish settlements. Apart from hemming in the Palestinians (and the director of the centre did not have right of access and travel on Israeli soil), the building of the wall, roads and settlements encroached on Palestinian land, cutting people off from their farmland and olive groves that were their traditional sources of income. In another conversation with a Christian leader in the West Bank I was hearing of his and his family's personal harassment by the Israeli authorities and the difficulties being faced by Palestinian Christians. Neither the director nor the Christian leader could see the overall situation improving. What, I asked, sustained them as they faced these very demanding situations? Their reply was the same: hope. Christian hope is not the same as optimism, where a person has a feeling that things will get better in the future. Hope is the knowledge that God does not desert his people in their darkest moments but brings them through to a new dawn. This knowledge is based on the way God has worked with his people in times past, even though there appears no way forward. Hope is most important for those in the most difficult situations.

Some of the finest demonstrations of hope are to be found in the book of Isaiah. In chapter 40 the prophet wants to bring hope to the people of Israel, who for several generations had been in exile in Babylon, far away from their beloved Jerusalem and fearful about whether they would ever return. They were desperate. The chapter builds up a picture of God as able to do the impossible and work miracles, even though it may be difficult to comprehend. All that is required is to hold on to hope in the trust that God is able to turn around even the most impossible situation:

> Have you not known? Have you not heard? The Lord is the everlasting God, the Creator of the ends of the earth. He does not faint or grow weary; his understanding is unsearchable. He gives power to the faint, and strengthens the powerless. Even youths will faint and be weary, and the young will fall exhausted; but those who wait for the Lord shall renew their strength, they shall mount up with wings like eagles, they shall run and not be weary, they shall walk and not faint. (Isa. 40.28–31)

Hope is important in reconciliation. It connects the present situation with the belief that reconciliation has already been brought about between God and humanity and so brings encouragement. If reconciliation is already a reality, it is the task of those involved in reconciliation to uncover it and give it wings.

Hope brings joy in the pursuit of reconciliation because it brings the assurance that reconciliation is within reach. But imagination, courage and commitment are then required by all involved. Imagination gives permission for blue-sky thinking, for dreaming, for thinking differently, recognizing that life is not always in the places we have traditionally searched for it. The resurrection of Jesus Christ showed this. Courage is required – all involved in seeking reconciliation are required to take risks. It is also required in facing the conflicts and difficulties the journey will bring. Reconciliation cannot be uncovered unless participants are willing to move from their current position and be transformed. Finally there needs to be commitment to the journey of reconciliation. This is a commitment to the belief that in every context, reconciliation – in Christ – is there to be uncovered. It is also a commitment to enable the growth and flourishing of others involved in the journey.

Hope is the vehicle that contains and enables the actual journeying towards reconciliation.

Reconciliation, power and vulnerability

In the highlighting of reconciliation as a gift it was made clear that no one party has control of reconciliation and that all parties need to regard themselves as equal partners in its pursuit (see Chapter 2). For this to happen, any environment where reconciliation is being sought needs to be strong and secure enough to contain vulnerability and struggle. Jesus Christ, God's embodiment of reconciliation, laid aside his power in order to bring about reconciliation:

> Let the same mind be in you that was in Christ Jesus, who, though he was in the form of God, did not regard equality with God as something to be exploited, but emptied himself, taking the form of a slave, being born in human likeness. And being found in human form, he humbled himself and became obedient to the point of death – even death on a cross. (Phil. 2.5–8)

Often vulnerability and struggle are regarded as signs of weakness rather than of humanity, with which faith traditions collude by expressing belief in ways that sanitize and make these risky and unpredictable elements safe. One of the refreshing aspects of Pope Francis' ministry is his admission that he has made mistakes and has been wrong in his decision making. Yet to admit to one's faults and vulnerabilities in public in the insecurity of the present age is to expose oneself to criticism and exploitation.

All pursuing reconciliation are called on to be countercultural by laying aside power rather than holding it tightly to themselves, and to be willing to be vulnerable.

Reconciliation and ritual

Reconciliation is confirmed, celebrated and strengthened by ritual. When peoples engaged in destructive conflict are reconciled there are usually the rituals of signing a treaty and a celebration meal. When there is a reconciliation between families in dispute in Arab cultures the chiefs of the families will shake hands and drink coffee together. Someone making a formal confession – sometimes referred to as a sacrament of reconciliation – to a Christian priest will have her or his reconciliation with God confirmed by words of forgiveness and blessing.

For Christians the Eucharist is the ritual most expressive of God's reconciliation with humanity. It is the sacrament of reconciliation. It confirms the reconciliation already brought about between God and humanity. It celebrates the fact of reconciliation and strengthens all those participating in their resolve to be a community of reconciliation and ambassadors of reconciliation in the world.

The Eucharist is a model for reconciliation. Women and men are summoned to this meal by God himself, who sets the tone and atmosphere for reconciliation. At the heart of the meal is thanksgiving – 'Eucharist' means thanksgiving – and praise for what God has done for the whole of creation through Jesus Christ and the work of the Holy Spirit. All those who wish to come to God's meal are required to be in good relationship and reconciled with their neighbour. They are required to be reconciled with God and within themselves by acknowledging their vulnerabilities and mistakes and confessing them. As they enter into the heart of the worship they bring with them, in addition to themselves and each other, the worlds in which they live. They pray, through the intercessions, for the wider world, their own communities, the Church, the sick and those who have died, that they may be fully part of the reconciliation. When the worshippers receive the bread and wine, now transformed into the body and blood of Jesus Christ, they are making themselves vulnerable to be transformed themselves. They are strengthened to be agents of reconciliation in the world and communities in which they spend their lives. 'Go in peace to love and serve the Lord' are the words with which they are sent out. 'In the name of Christ. Amen', they acclaim.

And finally

This chapter and Chapter 2, which focuses on five drivers of reconciliation (memory, victimhood, forgiveness, otherness and gift), are particularly closely related because the response to the one will affect the shaping of the other. For example, the way a person or people will have experienced and shown forgiveness will shape the way they view and handle conflict; conversely, the way they handle conflict may affect the way they view forgiveness. Similarly a person's or people's understanding of victimhood will influence how vulnerable they are willing to make themselves; conversely, their experience of vulnerability and whether it leads to reconciliation will affect their view and response to victimhood.

Having begun to weave, in the foregoing chapters, a tapestry of reconciliation, the following three chapters explore what a reconciling life, a reconciling church and a reconciling society may look like. There will not be a slavish following of a particular format, but the connections with what has gone before should be apparent.

For individual, quiet reflection

1 If storytelling is important both for the one who tells and those who hear, what stories could you tell about the pattern of your life that might benefit others, and which have had the greatest impact on you?
2 Think about moments of reconciliation in your life – maybe reconciliation with others, within yourself, in the community, between nations or with the environment. Do any of the marks of reconciliation highlighted in this chapter reflect your experience?
3 What occasions of thanksgiving have marked your own journey? Have the most memorable been for personal

achievement, family events, moments of national or international commemoration? And have you ever felt you ought to offer thanks but for some reason found yourself unable to do so?

For discussion in groups

1 Discuss occasions when seeking reconciliation has brought conflict.
2 'Suffering produces endurance, and endurance produces character, and character produces hope, and hope does not disappoint us' (Rom. 5.3–5). How crucial is hope in situations of reconciliation? What remains to be done if hope disappears?
3 Tell some stories about reconciliation that have been encouraging and inspiring.
4 Discuss occasions when reconciliation has been deepened through celebration and thanksgiving.

Prayer

God, you are enthroned in splendour, yet you are with us
always and everywhere:
we see you day by day in this world of your creation,
in its sights and sounds, its colour and its music;
we glimpse you in sacrament and prayer through the eye of faith,
and we meet your Son in those whom we encounter on our
Christian journey.
We pray that, as we look to find Christ in others,
so others may find him in us –
one God in Trinity, Father, Son and Holy Spirit. Amen.

Derek Carpenter

4

A reconciling life

Joel Salatin is an eco-farmer in Virginia who has developed 'forgiveness farming', a farming method that flies in the face of the industrial farming that has dominated the northern hemisphere over the last 60 years. In an account of the emotional toll that industrial farming was placing on so many farmers (and the high rate of depression among farmers in the UK will confirm that this is not a problem confined to the USA), Salatin gives the following account:

> An eco-farmer once told me that he quit industrial farming when he realized that his first waking thought every morning was, 'I wonder what's died up there in the hog house today?' He couldn't hear the birds chirping. He couldn't enjoy the sunrise, or the rainbow after a thunderstorm. And his kids wanted nothing to do with the farm.
>
> But after this epiphany, he closed down the pig concentration camp and devoted himself to pasture-based farming. Suddenly his children wanted to be involved. His thoughts turned lofty. He developed a can-do spirit. His emotional zest returned.[1]

Leaving to one side the use of theological symbolism in this account ('forgiveness farming'; 'epiphany'), the eco-farmer turned his back on industrial farming in search of reconciliation with creation, his children, possibly with God ('His thoughts turned lofty'), but certainly within himself ('His emotional zest returned').

This chapter explores, in the light of the preceding chapters, what a reconciling life may look like. Note the use of the phrase 'reconciling life' rather than 'reconciled life'. Although God has already reconciled himself to humanity, humanity has not yet fully grasped the fact and so is in the process of reconciling rather than already being reconciled. As has already been stated, reconciliation is a quest and journey that will not be completed in this life. We are works in progress, not the finished article.

Also, reconciling people attract others and frequently form communities of reconciliation, just as the eco-farmer attracted back his children who wanted to be involved in what became a source of new energy, life and hope. It will be shown in the next chapter that Christian churches are, at their best, communities of reconciliation, and when they fulfil this vocation they will attract others – conversely, when they fail to do so they will not. So 'reconciling' is used as a reminder that while humanity is still involved in the process of reconciliation, we may also be reconcilers at the same time.

Celebration and thanksgiving

Dancing in the Streets, a book by Barbara Ehrenreich, a journalist and historian of human behaviour, tells the story of joy and celebration.[2] The book focuses on the UK and the western world but takes the reader back to the ancient roots of ecstasy and ranges widely by drawing insights from a variety of cultures. In the chapter 'Jesus and Dionysus', Ehrenreich traces the relationship between Christian and pagan beliefs, specifically the beliefs and practices that developed around Dionysus, the deity of wine, dance and ecstatic states. Ehrenreich illustrates some lows and highs in the relationship.[3] For example, Jesus' insistence that he was the 'true vine' (John 15.1) suggests there must have been a false vine. The false vine may well have been Dionysus, on whom the passage from John could be regarded as a direct attack. On the other hand there are indications from the second and third centuries that there was a closer relationship between the deified Jesus Christ and Dionysus. In one instance Dionysus – who is identified by name – is portrayed hanging from a cross and in another is depicted on a fresco in a Christian burial site.[4]

In early and medieval times, people's natural exuberance found shape and expression through the festivals of the Church. Certainly dancing in churches was allowed and even enjoyed in the late Middle Ages. This was not always an easy relationship. There was the ever-present danger that celebrating, lubricated and fuelled by locally brewed ale, would spill over into unruly behaviour, and when that happened church officials, seeking to balance piety with riotous behaviour, had to try to bring some order into the celebrations. Generally, however, church members and its clergy were out there dancing and celebrating with the best of them.

The party-poopers of the day tended to be the civil authorities and ruling classes, who were anxious for two reasons. First, there was concern about social order. Second, there was a deeper concern that celebrating was potentially anarchic because it lifted the people temporarily out of their humdrum, dreary existence brought about by long working hours and little reward, and gave them a glimpse of what relationships and socializing could be like. The people experienced social and political liberation while the rulers feared civil disobedience. The story of dancing and celebration took a turn for the worse when the Church's theology joined forces with the political philosophy of the ruling classes at the Reformation and public celebration became less acceptable. There were a number of streams of thinking that brought this about, but one contributing factor was the breakdown of communal faith practices. A strong community and social life had developed around the rites and practices of the celebration of the saints. When the veneration of the saints became frowned upon and eventually banned, the social structures collapsed and were not replaced.[5]

Sadly the situation has not improved and, apart from momentary gleams of light, society has generally become more miserable, self-obsessed and fearful. Urbanization, the lure of the computer screen and the rise of a competitive market-based economy and its accompanying pressures have encouraged an environment where individualism gives momentum to a spiralling isolationism. When this is linked to a climate where festivities are discouraged or even banned, there will be a negative effect on the mental and spiritual health of the people. In places society has lost the art of corporate celebration and learnt that of over-indulgence or bingeing. Depression, regarded as the second most disabling illness across the globe, becomes more prominent, and apart from its direct effects it exacerbates other illnesses. There is no evidence to suggest that depression – or melancholy as it was known before the twentieth century – is a phenomenon of the modern era, though there is some that communal celebration and festivities help alleviate it. In his book *The Social Psychology of Leisure*, Professor Michael Argyle argues that the greatest source of joy is dancing.[6] So the dilemma is, as Barbara Ehrenreich succinctly expresses it: 'The immense tragedy for Europeans, I have argued, and most acutely for the northern Protestants among them, was that the same social forces that disposed them to depression also swept away a traditional cure.'[7]

Celebration is in the diet of the reconciling person. The theological emphasis within celebration is praise and thanksgiving. There is the praise of God and thanksgiving for what God has done because of his love for humanity. Praise and thanksgiving are radical and politically subversive acts because they are acts directed to God, who is more powerful and influential than the rulers of this world. Therefore the more people celebrate in this way, the less this world has power over them and over their allegiances.

Praise gains its highest expression in the psalms, where God's authority, kingship and otherness are firmly asserted:

> The LORD is king! Let the earth rejoice; let the many coastlands be glad! Clouds and thick darkness are all around him; righteousness and justice are the foundation of his throne. Fire goes before him, and consumes his adversaries on every side. His lightnings light up the world; the earth sees and trembles.
> (Ps. 97.1–4)

The other form of celebration is thanksgiving to God for ways he has saved in the past and continues to save today. Again, the psalms are full of thanksgiving: 'O give thanks to the LORD, call on his name, make known his deeds among the peoples. Sing to him, sing praises to him; tell of all his wonderful works' (Ps. 105.1–2). And the thanksgiving is closely associated to remembering what God has done for his people in the past: 'Remember the wonderful works he has done, his miracles, and the judgements he has uttered' (Ps. 105.5).

Relating thanksgiving with remembering what God has done in the past is at the heart of the Holy Communion service or Eucharist (which, as noted earlier, means 'thanksgiving'). The Eucharistic Prayer tells the story of God's activity among his people and his drawing closer to them, particularly in the person of Jesus Christ. For all this, worshippers give thanks. At the beginning of the Prayer the priest says, 'Let us give thanks to the Lord our God.' The people then reply, 'It is right to give thanks and praise.' The rest of the Prayer lists reasons for giving thanks to God, highlighting God's love for humanity despite humanity's constantly turning its back on God:

You fashioned us in your image
and placed us in the garden of your delight.
Though we chose the path of rebellion
you would not abandon your own.

Again and again you drew us into your covenant of grace.

The climax of the thanksgiving is in the sending of Jesus Christ:

Lord God, you are the most holy one,
enthroned in splendour and light,
yet in the coming of your son Jesus Christ
you reveal the power of your love
made perfect in our human weakness.[8]

In this way worshippers are lifted from the world in which they reside into the world where God saves, restores and liberates. Worship can liberate because worshippers view their circumstances differently – they do not simply learn about reconciled life in God in a cerebral way but also glimpse and experience it. Worship refreshes the soul, giving sustenance to continue the journey. Whenever we praise God, something is awoken within us that helps towards an inner reconciliation.

The authenticity of celebrating, praising and giving thanks to God can be tested in the way relationships in this world are transformed. Relationships with those around us come to be viewed differently. Celebrating becomes an important way of deepening and enjoying the love of family, friends and community. Just as celebrating feeds our relationship with God, in a similar way other relationships are fed. Salatin's eco-farmer would hear the birds chirping, he would enjoy the rainbow, his children and others would be attracted and want to be involved and his thoughts would 'turn lofty'. All of which are markers of the reconciling life.

The point has already been made that celebrating is important from the perspective of the mental health of individuals and communities, and from here the Christian faith has something to teach a society that has either too little celebration or too much, ending up bingeing. Christian communities have joy and rejoicing as part of their DNA and so they have a role in modelling to society how to enjoy life. When distinguishing Christian behaviour from that of their pagan counterparts the third century Christian author Tertullian wrote, 'See how these Christians love one another.' It would be a tribute if somebody could say of twenty-first-century Christians, 'See how these Christians celebrate and enjoy themselves.'

Focusing beyond the self

A fear of and concern about the 'other' whom we consider a threat to our security or, in a difficult economic climate, a risk to our jobs, mean we live at a time when self-centredness is a feature of society. Human beings are not naturally self-centred and self-possessed and can be seen to rise above and beyond themselves in heroic ways. The centenary of the beginning of the First World War, marked in 2014, is a reminder of the heights of heroism to which ordinary people can aspire. But so much within contemporary society encourages us to look at our own needs in isolation of others – there is a focus on taking rather than giving. It speaks about fairness rather than justice. Fairness is a judgement about right and wrong when everybody starts from a level playing field; it is concerned to find equilibrium when balancing one claim against another; it is blind to the fact that some, through no choice of their own, find themselves in material poverty, others, again through no choice of their own, in material wealth. Justice, on the other hand, has morality and ethics at its heart and recognizes that there are inequalities in society.[9]

In contemporary society we have lost perspective in that we place more value on celebrities than on heroes. Celebrities are people who display talent, becoming famous and often rich for what they do and the way they do it. They tend to focus on their image and are fed by publicity. We watch their downfall with a certain amount of pained glee, often disappointed that public trust has been betrayed but quietly glad to see that they too have feet of clay.

Heroes do not usually become rich and are not always famous. They are not concerned about public opinion and are willing to risk everything, even their lives, in pursuit of what they believe to be right. The causes they advocate are not usually their own but reflect values to which they aspire. The downfall of a hero is catastrophic for those who look up to him or her, but a real hero will always rise again, no matter how long it takes.

The reconciling life looks beyond the self. We have already seen that Michael Argyle, in *The Social Psychology of Leisure*, argues that dancing is the greatest source of human joy. Argyle believes that the second greatest source of joy is volunteering. In essence volunteering is a social activity geared at helping the community and the other. It is a focusing beyond the self.

The Church of England's Prayer book, *Common Worship*, encourages worshippers to begin the day with their minds raised beyond themselves. At the beginning of Morning Prayer, worshippers pray: 'As we rejoice in the gift of this new day, so may the light of your presence, O God, set our hearts on fire with love for you; now and for ever.'[10]

Looking beyond oneself, turning one's thoughts 'lofty' (as the newly converted eco-farmer confirmed), is another marker of the reconciling life.

Listening and finding a voice to tell one's story

In his book *Christianity Rediscovered* the catholic missionary Vincent Donovan tells of his remarkable work among the Masai tribes of East Africa.[11] Donovan was called to a Catholic mission station with its hospital and school with a zeal to evangelize. He quickly realized that though he fulfilled the traditional duties of a missionary through teaching and evangelism, he was not reaching the cultural soul of the Masai. Seven years after the establishment of the mission station there was no indication that Christian faith was mentioned or practised once the people had stepped outside its gates. So with his bishop's agreement he wanted to approach his task in a different way.

Donovan went away from the mission station into the bush and lived among the nomadic Masai. He did not try to evangelize in the traditional way but asked the Masai to tell him their story. He listened intently. They told of the wanderings of their ancestors over the generations, and Donovan could see a link with the wanderings of the people of Israel. The Masai saw Donovan's interest in their story and the deep respect with which he listened, and asked him to tell them his story. He told them the Christian story, starting with Abraham, where there were resonances with the Masai experience, and leading up to Jesus Christ. They were so moved that they asked to be baptized.

Donovan listened. He listened to the story of the Masai, to their culture and their environment, and found where it converged with his. He also listened in other ways – deep within himself, thinking about his own personal story and the story of the Christian faith as he had received it. And he listened to the directions in which he believed God was calling him, constantly 'testing' this call in the light of how God had spoken in the past (through Scripture and tradition), had been speaking through the stories of the Masai and continued to speak through them and their culture. Through this process of listening and adjusting stories in the light of what he had heard, Donovan was able to find the right 'voice' to speak into the depths of the Masai soul.

Those living the reconciling life are in touch with the narrative of their own lives and, through listening and dialogue, able to find the voice to speak into the context in which they find themselves.

Inner reconciliation

With whom do people seeking inner reconciliation wish to be reconciled? Do people who are fully reconciled within themselves exist? Have they ever existed? What about Jesus Christ?

The first of these questions will be addressed below, but first we explore the questions around the 'reconciled person'.

The Church views Jesus as fully human and fully God. Theologians over the centuries went to great lengths to prove Jesus' full humanity, though there are differences of emphasis. While St John's Gospel shows Jesus as a man with a stature and presence that are rarely ruffled (except in John 11.35, where he weeps at the death of his friend Lazarus), St Luke says that he 'grew and became strong, filled with wisdom, and the favour of God was upon him' (2.40), and the rest of his Gospel shows Jesus growing and struggling. The letter to the Hebrews makes it clear that Jesus shared humanity completely, except in the way he was without sin (Heb. 4.15). Any watering down of the full humanity of Christ undermined the self-giving of God on the cross and the love God has for his children. Unless God could fully identify with humanity, his death and resurrection would be undervalued and rendered ineffective.

But what does it mean to be reconciled within ourselves? Does it mean experiencing a warm inner glow and exuding happiness? Does it mean no longer struggling and no longer being tempted? This was not the experience of Jesus Christ nor of some of his most devoted followers.

Jesus experienced inner conflict at the beginning of his earthly ministry, when he faced temptations in the wilderness, and towards the end, when he struggled with his imminent arrest and death in the garden of Gethsemane (Matt. 4.1ff. and 26.36ff.). We have already seen in the life of Antony of Egypt that inner conflict increased the more deeply he became embroiled with God. Amma Sarah, one of the Desert Mothers, was said for 13 years to have 'waged warfare against the demon of fornication'. She never prayed that the warfare should cease but she said, 'O God, give me strength.'[12] The presence of her temptations and the struggle against them made her aware that she was truly alive. The sixteenth-century Spanish mystic Teresa of Avila reflects the experience of Antony of Egypt in that she recognized that the closer she got to God in prayer and the more space is given to God, the more one notices the conflicts, compulsions, desires, vanities and fantasies kept at bay by the ordinary activity of the conscious mind. She believed that what is in the conscious mind may tell us little of what is in the depths of the self. The imagination may run riot but if our life and being are turned towards God, this does not matter.

These spiritual giants are showing that the more deeply they are drawn into a relationship with God, the more they become aware of their human frailty. The more they become aware of their human frailty, the more they can apprehend and need to rely on God's unconditional love and forgiveness. These lives have periods of doubt, difficulty and sometimes of depression. The joyful saint, Francis of Assisi, struggled with depression and a sense of failure throughout his life. It was discovered after her death that another Theresa, Mother Theresa of Calcutta, went through a period of darkness and doubt in her last illness. St Dominic, the founder of the Dominican order, was a joyful person who laughed most of the day but wept most of the night. However, they all believed that the goal towards which they strove – that is, reconciliation with God – was the only route they could take to be true to themselves and their calling as children of God. They all displayed a number of marks of reconciliation, one of which is that they attracted communities of reconciliation around themselves.

The saints teach us that reconciling with God will not remove struggles, conflict and doubts within; rather it is more likely they will increase – the quest for reconciliation will bring a deeper joy that may not be felt but will be apparent by the way it fosters relationships with other reconcilers and others seeking reconciliation.

So we now return to the first question posed at the beginning of this section: 'With whom do people seeking inner reconciliation wish to be reconciled?' Seeking that elusive inner reconciliation is bound up with being in creative dialogue within ourselves, constantly being in touch with who we are becoming and the world in which we are living. At the same time, for the Christian, the quest for inner reconciliation cannot be seen in isolation from the quest for reconciliation with the God who has already reconciled himself to us.

Vulnerability

There is a general belief in society that to be vulnerable is to be weak and therefore avoided at all costs. In some walks of life, displaying vulnerability, admitting to mistakes and acknowledging woundedness render people incapable of doing their jobs. The politician, the chief executive of a hospital trust, the managing director of a company display vulnerability at their peril. Yet depth and growth can only come through vulnerability. Rather than being a sign of weakness, acknowledging vulnerability is one of strength, opening people up to new possibilities and new hope.

One of the most vulnerable times in the history of Israel was during their time in the desert. Released from Egypt by a reluctant Pharaoh, they had left their homes and belongings, persuaded by Moses to relinquish a life of slavery for the freedom God had in store for them. But the desert was a tough place. They frequently looked back with nostalgia towards Egypt, where they had been slaves, complaining that it was better to be alive and slaves than march in hunger and uncertainty towards freedom. It was one of the most difficult times in their history.

They were at their most vulnerable in the inhospitable and unfamiliar desert environment, at the mercy of people there they did not know. Yet they later looked back to their time in the desert as formative when they rediscovered their calling as the people of God. So significant was this difficult period of vulnerability in their formation that they decided to remember it yearly in the Feast of Tabernacles (or Tents), a major Festival of the Jewish year, when they would erect tents outside their settled homes in which to spend time looking back to this period of vulnerability. This Feast is still observed today, and anybody visiting Israel at the right time in late autumn will see rough tents erected outside Jewish homes – including blocks of flats – to remind Jews of the deep and lasting significance of this time in their history.

One of the marks of a reconciling life is a willingness to acknowledge vulnerability, recognizing that it is not possible to be perfect in everything, that everyone is bound to make wrong choices and wrong decisions and carries around wounds from the past. The good news at the heart of the Christian faith is that far from holding a person back, vulnerabilities placed in the hand of God help one move forward more quickly in the journey of reconciliation. In a talk that he gave, a violin repairer said that a well-made violin that has had to be repaired will produce a better sound than before it was broken. All of humanity has been well made by God, and so this offers hope to all. Let us explore in more detail that it is not possible to be perfect, that everyone makes mistakes and carries wounds from the past.

First, it is not possible to be perfect in everything. While everyone has strengths, so too have they limitations. Someone gifted in sport may be a disaster at DIY. The skilled carpenter may be unable to teach his skills to others. The person who can naturally communicate with those society rejects may find he or she cannot work with those who are more established and comfortable. Limitations, like vulnerabilities, are marks of humanity, and it is important for us to make friends with and be kind to our limitations rather than view them as flaws in character and pretend they do not exist. There is a powerful current within contemporary British society that finds it difficult to recognize and cope with the human reality of limitations and vulnerabilities, hence a strong emphasis on achievement and results. Of course achievement and results are to be recognized and celebrated, but when they are viewed in a culture that spurns and, at a deep level, is fearful of limitations and vulnerabilities, then they are deified and their celebration can be divisive rather than cohesive. The psychoanalyst Stephen Grosz provides a surprising example of the problem this can create.

As Grosz was collecting his daughter from nursery school he overheard the nursery assistant praising Grosz's daughter for a tree she had drawn. 'Wow, you really are an artist', said the assistant. Giving such praise is not at all unusual and fits in with the popular belief that praise, self-confidence and academic performance are closely related.[13] If we are praised for what we have done, it follows that we become more self-confident and will reach even greater heights. It is not uncommon for children to be praised for work that is not particularly good in the belief this will encourage them in their next efforts. But research over the last ten years has concluded that praising children as clever or gifted may cause them to under-perform rather than do better. Children may well react by thinking they need do no more because what they have done has already attracted so much praise and approval. Furthermore there is evidence that children praised for their cleverness develop worries about failing – they had their reputation to sustain, and there was a subsequent loss of self-esteem. Many will also be aware that despite the praise, what they did was not as 'perfect' as it was made out to be. Also, when confronted with new tasks they tend to opt for those they already know.

However, research has also shown that children praised for their effort – rather than their achievement – were sufficiently flexible to try new approaches in order to do better next time. They also demonstrated an inner resilience, recognizing that their efforts were more important than their shortcomings and that they could improve on these. This also meant that their achievements were not viewed in isolation but alongside their shortcomings and the importance of their effort.

Second, people are bound to make wrong choices and wrong decisions. Again, it is part of being human. The Bible is teeming with examples of people who, for a variety of reasons but all relating back to their humanity, made mistakes. Nevertheless God did not in the end give up on them. Jacob was a cheat, a liar and a trickster: he cunningly enticed his brother Esau to give him his birthright, deceived his father Isaac and lied to him by disguising himself and pretending to be Esau (in this way receiving the blessing Isaac had reserved for the older brother), trumped the cunning of his father-in-law Laban by ensuring he had a larger proportion of his flocks than Laban intended (Gen. 25.29ff.; 27.1ff.; 30.31ff.). Israel, as a people, turned away from God in the wilderness, and when they had been settled in the land promised by God they twice more turned away (Exod. 32.1ff.; Amos 5.21ff.; Jer. 5.1ff.).

In the New Testament, Peter, who promised to follow Jesus to his death, lost his nerve and denied ever knowing him. After being restored and forgiven by Jesus on the shores of Galilee, Peter was recognized as one of the main leaders of the fledgling Church. But in this capacity he was accused by St Paul of hypocrisy and double standards when he changed his attitude towards the Gentiles under pressure from Jewish traditionalists. Peter was the rock on which the Church was to be built and Jesus tells him that 'the gates of Hades will not prevail against it' (Matt. 16.18). Many clergy are ordained priest and deacon around the day on which St Peter is celebrated (29 June), which is a reminder that Christian ministers are both divinely called and humanly fallible. The very Paul who accused Peter of hypocrisy and double standards himself admitted to being a persecutor of the Church – he who more than anybody else pointed out the significance of reconciliation in the Christian tradition at one time struck fear in the hearts of those following the way of Christ (Matt. 26.69ff.; John 21.15ff.; Matt. 16.18ff.; Gal. 2.11ff.; Phil. 3.3b–6; Acts 9.13).

This litany of human beings with their weaknesses and foibles is a reminder that God's purposes are brought about through human beings who, like all human beings, make wrong choices and wrong decisions. Their stories also indicate that it is possible for people who have made mistakes to be transformed. Transformation does not mean they will never make mistakes again but it can teach people that if they rely too much on themselves they can easily stray from the right path. When they do stray, others may suffer as a result. This has always happened and, since God can only work through human beings, it always will happen.

Systems of encouragement, support and discipline can provide a framework in which Christians – lay and ordained – can live their calling, and at their best the role of such systems is to enable ministry to flourish for witnessing to the reconciling God in the world. Sometimes the wrong choices and wrong decisions can be destructive, so that not just the Church but also society is required to have a role in judging the offence and balancing the risk posed. It is worth remembering that many of the examples from the Bible would have been regarded as offences under church rules – yet they are seen as essential building stones for the platform from which God's reconciling love can be promoted. Those who carried them out were instruments through which God could work. In some instances – and this was a point made in relation to St Paul in Chapter 1 – their lives mirrored the reconciling love and forgiveness of God.

In a society that is permissive but not forgiving, a reconciling life needs to recognize and accept the vulnerability and limitations of humanity – with our tendency to make wrong choices and wrong decisions – and place this alongside the human, God-given potential to rise above the restrictions the world tries to impose.

Finally, each person carries around wounds from the past. In 2012 Britain had a number of celebrations, but as already mentioned in Chapter 2, one of the high points was the Olympic and Paralympic Games. The magnificent opening ceremony set an atmosphere and tone of a healthy balance between effort and achievement that was maintained throughout the summer. What made that period so special was that athletes who had major disabilities, some from birth, others through trauma, were able to transcend their limitations to achieve athletic prowess of which many so-called able-bodied people could only dream. Although the paralympians faced physical limitations, psychologically and spiritually they viewed themselves as differently abled rather than disabled. From a spectator's perspective, one gained the impression the paralympians viewed their skills as different from rather than inferior to those of their fellow Olympians. They resolutely refused the role of the victim.

To a greater or lesser extent everybody carries wounds from the past. They may be physical, psychological or spiritual or a combination of all three. One frequently hears of a physical trauma that brings psychological and spiritual distress. Post-traumatic stress disorder, a problem for troops returning from a war zone, may have had a physical catalyst in what was experienced during or after battle, but the intensity of the physical experience usually has psychological symptoms. If somebody is attacked in the street or is robbed at home, the trauma may well be manifested psychologically. Conversely, psychological trauma can have physical symptoms. Negative stress can bring about heart disorders or rashes on parts of the body. Spiritual intensity, such as regular focus on the suffering of Christ, may affect the body physically. A number of saints, including St Francis of Assisi, are said to have had the marks of Christ's wounds – the stigmata – on their body. Woundedness, which is part of vulnerability, is also a feature of being human. Human beings may have no say about the wounds inflicted on them but men and women have a choice in the ways they respond. First, they have a choice about recognizing their woundedness. If, either through intent or ignorance, we do not acknowledge that we have been wounded, there is a possibility that the wound cannot be healed and a danger that the same wound will be inflicted on others as well as ourselves. Whereas if the wound is acknowledged it can be healed and become a source of healing for others. Scars will remain, and where there are scars it is possible that the wound will break open because the area remains vulnerable. But when wounds are regarded in this way, life can never be the same again. When Jesus appeared to the disciples after his resurrection they recognized him through his scars and wounds (John 20.19, 25). St John's Gospel emphasized that it was through Jesus' woundedness that health and healing came to the world (19.34).

A reconciling life recognizes and acknowledges woundedness as part of its vulnerability, but woundedness is seen not as a barrier to reconciliation, rather as a fast-track towards it. St Paul should have the last word on woundedness. He writes about a 'thorn in the flesh' that was given to him that made him boast, not on his own behalf, but of his weakness:

> Three times I appealed to the Lord about this, that it would leave me, but he said to me, 'My grace is sufficient for you, for power is made perfect in weakness.' So I will boast all the more gladly of my weaknesses, so that the power of Christ may dwell in me. Therefore I am content with weaknesses, insults, hardships, persecutions, and calamities for the sake of Christ: whenever I am weak, then I am strong. (2 Cor. 12.8–10)

For individual, quiet reflection

1 Read and reflect on the Eucharistic Prayers in *Common Worship*, the Book of Common Prayer or the Communion Prayers used at your church. Which do you find the most helpful in assisting you to glimpse and experience reconciled life? The *Common Worship* Eucharistic Prayers can be found online at <www.churchofengland.org/prayer-worship/worship/texts/principal-services/holy-communion/epsforonefront.aspx>.

2 Who have been particular heroes for you in your personal life, and what has marked them out from others who have influenced you? What parts of their lives give you cause for real thanksgiving in your personal prayers?

3 Just as celebrating feeds our relationship with God, in a similar way other relationships are fed. Do celebrating, praising and giving thanks to God on a regular basis affect your relationship with those around?

For discussion in groups

1 If 'forgiveness farming' can bring reconciliation and inner harmony, in which other areas of secular life can such a concept be brought to bear? In politics, in banking? And what might this mean for relationships?
2 What aspects of Christian life and faith cause you to 'dance in the streets'?
3 Reference has been made to the Eucharistic Prayers, with quotations from Prayer F. Compare the other Eucharistic Prayers and consider how they demonstrate that God saves, restores and liberates.
4 The year 2014 marks 100 years since the outbreak of the First World War. Is there cause for celebration amid the commemoration?
5 In the book *The Social Psychology of Leisure*, dancing and volunteering are considered the greatest sources of human joy. Is this your experience?
6 The desert is a barren place to our human understanding but it is also a fruitful place in spiritual terms. How can we make some sort of 'desert place' practically within our homes and, more important, within our hearts – a place where the world is silenced and where the beauty and barrenness of the desert merge together?

Prayer

When pride takes precedence over humility,
  Father, forgive.
When greed sings louder than generosity.
  Father, forgive.

When wealth grinds others into poverty,
  Father, forgive.
When injustice triumphs over integrity,
  Father, forgive.
When acceptance gives way to prejudice,
  Father, forgive.
When bigotry breeds intolerance,
  Father, forgive.
When selfishness defeats the common good,
  Father forgive –
and bring healing, wholeness and peace to a broken world,
  through your Son who reconciles all things to himself
  and in whose name we pray. Amen.

Derek Carpenter

5
A reconciling church

The Church is called to be what the world would look like if it were in touch with God through Jesus Christ. Its role is to strive joyfully and assiduously towards this calling. At the same time it needs to recognize that while there will be glimpses of glory that will be encouragements, it will not reach fulfilment in this world but needs to be always open to being renewed and reformed – and renewal and reformation will always come from outside the establishment.[1] One of the treasures given to the 'clay jars' that make up the Church is the gift of reconciliation (2 Cor. 4.7). One way the Church can gauge whether it is being faithful to its calling is by the extent to which it is a reconciling community. How far is its life being fed by the reconciliation God has already achieved through Jesus Christ? Is this being reflected by relationships within and beyond the church community? This chapter reflects on these issues through the lenses of culture, relationships and authority – all matters at the heart of St Paul's stormy relationship with the Corinthian Church in the first century. It will then look at reconciling communities emerging from churches and finally consider the role of worship in reconciliation and transformation. It is not possible to have a reconciling church without reconciling worship.

When someone talks about the church, which church is meant? For churchgoers it is most probably the local church they attend. The understanding of those who have a church in their community that they do not attend will come from the way they were treated when they wanted their baby baptized or wanted to get married, or from seeing the local minister conduct a funeral either at the church or local crematorium. The attitudes and behaviour of known church members in the community will influence the way people view the church. They will also form an understanding of the church from the way it is looked after and presented to the community. Are its doors always locked and bolted? That will send out a significant message about welcome. Churches that have replaced dark wooded doors with glass doors transform the way a church is viewed, especially by those who do not attend. Locked doors say 'Keep out!' Glass doors encourage people to come closer to peer in.

Others with little or no experience of the church may think of the institution, the Church of England – what might come to mind are wealth, bishops in the House of Lords, remoteness and being out of touch. But the 'church' is not always the church with the tower surrounded by a churchyard in the community or city centre.

There are churches in hospitals, psychiatric units, schools, universities, armed services, airports, shopping centres and prisons, though they are usually referred to as chaplaincies. Some do not have a regular place for worship but may have to use a classroom or a quiet room. These 'churches', which may have only a few worshippers, are as important as traditional churches. Chaplaincies have a sharp focus on reconciliation because chaplaincy ministry will usually have a strong pastoral component, where people will be seeking an inner reconciliation. Chaplaincies are pioneering churches in that they have regular, daily contact with people of other faiths and none and with people who are sympathetic and antagonistic to belief. Churches may not have a building and they do not need a specific geographical area – all they require is a worshipping community that witnesses to the faith to those with whom they come into contact. Such communities can meet in a house (as they did in St Paul's time), in a coffee shop or even a pub.

'Church' in this chapter can be any or all of these understandings. It could be the local church or the Church of England; it could be the church in the coffee shop or the church in the pub. But all of them should be reconciling churches both beyond and within themselves, and a sign of the depth to which they are living reconciliation is by the reconciling communities formed as a result of who they are.

A stormy relationship – Paul and the Church in Corinth

First-century Corinth was a vibrant and prosperous city strategically placed for trade with Asia and Italy. Its wealth came from agriculture, manufacturing and trading and its communities were multicultural, multifaith and socially diverse. It included Jewish refugees who had been expelled from Rome. In this cosmopolitan cauldron Paul fostered a young Church whose diversity reflected that of the city. There were men and women, rich people, tradespeople, slaves and former slaves. They had been followers of a variety of religions. There were around 200 followers of Christ in Corinth at the time of St Paul, some of whom owned large houses. Worship took place in house churches.

The challenge faced by Paul and the churches was holding together and reconciling diversity. Reading Paul's letters to the Christians in Corinth, three social groupings are apparent within the Church.

1 The first group was made up of wealthy and influential former slaves (the nouveau riche) – property owners in whose houses the Christians gathered. Crispus, a former chairman of the synagogue, belonged to this group.
2 The second and largest group was made up of uneducated slaves and dockers, many of them foreigners, and referred to as Chloe's people in Paul's letters. They complained that

they were not properly treated by other Christians because of their lowly status, and when they arrived at meetings there was little for them to eat because the better-off had arrived earlier and overindulged themselves.

3 The third group could be described as akin to a middle class. They were educated slaves, house slaves and scribes who worked for the Roman administration and for commerce. They would have been reluctant to be closely associated with the slaves and dockers (group 2) – they felt more comfortable with the wealthy former slaves (group 1), to whose status they aspired.

When the churches gathered together, those who were wealthy and influential in Corinthian society (group 1) assumed such status should be replicated in the Church. This would be akin to today's managing directors and chief executives expecting that by right they should be able to exercise the same influence in their church lives as in their professional lives, and that the Church should be organized and managed like their companies. Similarly the educated slaves (group 3) regarded themselves a higher class than the uneducated slaves (group 2) and closer to group 1. Groups 1 and 3 were educated and could therefore read the Scriptures, which would, in their eyes, give them leadership advantages over the illiterate slaves of group 2. In addition, in Roman society it was the men who made the decisions – the women were not expected to speak out in public.

So when Christians met in their churches there was a polarization between the wealthy and influential and the educated slaves on the one hand (groups 1 and 3) and the uneducated slaves (group 2) on the other. Groups 1 and 3 claimed that because they could read the scriptural texts, that gave them the right to interpret them in the light of the life and witness of Jesus Christ, thereby claiming superior knowledge about the faith. At the same time group 2 claimed that they did not need to be able to read them because the risen Christ communicated to them directly through visions, speaking in tongues and prophetic insights. Paul assured the Corinthian Christians that God worked through all of them regardless of their social, cultural and economic background, and that Christ spoke in different ways to people, regardless of their background and learning – one form of communication was not more important or theologically sound than another:

> To each is given the manifestation of the Spirit for the common good. To one is given through the Spirit the utterance of wisdom, and to another the utterance of knowledge according to the same Spirit, to another faith by the same Spirit, to another gifts of healing by the one Spirit, to another the working of miracles, to another prophecy, to another the discernment of spirits, to another various kinds of tongues, to another the interpretation of tongues. All these are activated by one and the same Spirit, who allots to each one individually just as the Spirit chooses. (1 Cor. 12.7–11)

While some (groups 1 and 3) tried to import the social, cultural and economic hierarchies that existed in society into the church community, others (group 2 and the women) resisted because one of the teachings of this new faith to which they were attracted was that all were regarded as equal in the eyes of God. Here was a question of justice. Unlike other religions, Jesus Christ had a particular appeal to the poor and marginalized. Paul's letter said as much:

> For just as the body is one and has many members, and all the members of the body, though many, are one body, so it is with Christ. For in the one Spirit we were all baptized into one body – Jews and Greeks, slaves or free – and we were all made to drink of one Spirit. (1 Cor. 12.12–13)

Paul was not denying cultural diversity, neither was he pretending that socio-economic distinctions did not exist, just as he was not pretending in his letter to the Galatians that there was no distinction between male or female (Gal. 3.28); rather he was relativizing the differences. These differences had previously been regarded as largely unbridgeable chasms because status or economic position depended on them. But now what was more important than all of these was a relationship with Jesus Christ, and in this relationship such distinctions were less significant. It would have been difficult for those with something to lose to hear and receive this, but a real joy to those who had nothing. Paul then went on (1 Cor. 12.14–26) to use the metaphor of the body to describe the relationship between the different groups.[2]

After the frustrations, appeals and warnings, and providing the image of the body to help the Corinthian Church understand how they should relate among themselves, Paul launches into poetry in chapter 13 with his famous passage on the importance of love. This passage did not come out of romantic musings but in the middle of a very stormy relationship.

In addition to being beset by socio-economic and cultural divisions there was also a factionalism that compromised the gospel. This is revealed in Paul's concern that Corinthian Christians claimed allegiance to different leaders, such as Apollos, Cephas, Paul or Christ (1 Cor. 1.11–12). Paul's overall concern was to reconcile the Christians in Corinth to each other. Their behaviour was an indication that their faith could not be rooted in Jesus Christ, God's embodiment of reconciliation, if they were not reconciled to each other.

Another concern of Paul's was the rejection of him by some of the Corinthians. This has already been hinted at when Corinthians allied themselves with particular leaders, but Corinthian rejection of Paul emerges frequently through both letters.[3] For Paul, rejection of him as God's ambassador was extremely serious – it was a rejection of God and another sign that the Corinthians were not reconciled to God.

Followers of Christ were being called to form radical, new communities that related together in new ways. When they were together they were not to allow their socio-economic and cultural divisions, which characterized the society in which they lived, to dominate their oneness in Christ; neither were they to allow them to dominate the running of the Christian community. They were not to be tempted into a factionalism by claiming to follow different leaders, and they were to recognize the authority of Paul, who had been given a particular role in relation to Gentile communities. Their failure to be reconciled in these ways indicated that they were not rooted in the reconciliation between God and humanity brought about by Christ.[4] The three areas can be translated today into culture, relationships and authority.

Culture

Ever since the time of Jesus the Christian faith has had the challenge of speaking into the heart of cultures. The Gospel writers tell us that Jesus Christ himself, shaped in first-century Palestine, spoke into the heart of people by communicating intuitively through the culture of his time. He healed the blind man in Bethsaida by putting saliva on his eyes and laying hands on him (Mark 8.22–26); he spoke about the kingdom of God using agricultural images (Mark 4.1–9); he used the story of a traditional wedding when telling people to be watchful (Matt. 25.1–13). But he is not afraid to issue challenges when religious and cultural understandings contradict what he is communicating. Against all the conventions, Jesus heals on the Sabbath (John 5.1–18); he asks a Samaritan woman for a drink at a well (John 4.7–10); he says that a woman caught in the act of adultery should go free (John 8.1–10); he eats in the house of Zacchaeus, a chief tax collector considered to be a sinner (Luke 19.1–10).

When the young faith crossed ethnic and religious frontiers, difficult decisions needed to be made. Once it was agreed that Gentiles could be invited into the communities of faith that had hitherto been dominated by Jews, a decision had to be made whether they first needed to become Jews to be recognized as Christian (Acts 15). We have already seen in this chapter the struggles Paul had when people from a variety of backgrounds and cultures wanted to become followers of Jesus Christ. In the early Church, Christian apologists tried to 'translate' the gospel, conceived in a Hebrew context, into a Greek and Hellenistic thought-world. Chapter 4 showed the issues faced by Vincent Donovan, a Catholic missionary working among the Masai of East Africa, when he tried to engage with the soul of those who were speaking with him. Communicating with the heart and soul of the culture is something at which Christians need constantly to work. There are some parts of the gospel that transcend words, such as the way Christians live and their treatment of others. But it is important to seek words and rituals that articulate the gospel afresh. It is also important to remember that God is already engaged in all cultures and peoples, though it may be the role of the Christian to point to God's activity. But what do we understand by culture?

The cultural anthropologist Clifford Geertz speaks of human beings as animals suspended in webs of significance they themselves have spun. 'Culture', which is what we make of the world materially, spiritually and intellectually, is the name for those webs.[5] In similar vein, the theologian Timothy Gorringe regards culture as being concerned with 'the spiritual, ethical and intellectual significance of the material world. It is, therefore, of fundamental theological concern.'[6] In addition, culture will have an effect on – though not always determine – a society's response to those phenomena it cannot control, such as birth, death and natural disasters. Culture provides a discipline where such phenomena are acknowledged as of fundamental importance in a society's self-understanding. Geertz and Gorringe provide helpful pointers to an understanding of culture in a world that is culturally diverse.

Culture is generally articulated through stories that remember the past, adopting a number of media such as narrative, song, art and ritual. All this is reconciled on a tapestry that enables a people to relate to the present both through the past and, in some instances, through visions for the future. Jewish culture is shaped with rituals, stories, song and art, some of which will be about the horrors of the Holocaust, persecution and victimhood. Palestinian culture is similarly shaped by stories, poems and experiences of constant movement and being unjustly driven from their ancestral lands. Culture can sustain a people facing trauma, providing them with resilience in difficult times. When the people of Israel were forced into the harshness of exile in Babylonia six centuries before Christ, it was a revisiting of their intellectual, spiritual and ethical roots – Gorringe's definition of culture – that sustained them and provided a basis for re-establishing their identity when they returned home.

In *Dancing in the No-Fly Zone* the journalist Hadani Ditmars writes of her visits to Iraq in some of its darkest times, in particular when the full effect of sanctions was being felt by its people in 1997 and after the US–British Invasion in 2003. Ditmars was amazed that amid battles and devastation the cultural life of the Iraqis flourished, sustaining their spirits. People celebrated marriages, drama flourished and, dodging the air raids, markets continued to trade.[7]

There are many cultures within any one society and Christians need to consider and engage critically with them all, alert to the fact that faith is itself shaped by culture. There are industrial, rural, working-class, managerial and postmodern cultures. There is high culture, mass culture and popular culture. There are pop and rock cultures.[8] However, in exploring cultures it is those that speak into the soul of the people, those able to sustain them at their most difficult times, that are particularly important, especially as far as reconciliation is concerned.

Some forms of culture are ephemeral, dehumanizing and infantilizing of the population – for example, mass culture which, linked to the world of celebrity and entertainment, has commercialism and gratification among its dominant features.[9] Neil Postman, Marshall McLuhan's successor at New York University, delivers what he describes as 'the Huxleyan warning' about such cultures:

> What Huxley teaches is that in the age of advanced technology, spiritual devastation is more likely to come from an enemy with a smiling face than from one whose countenance exudes suspicion and hate. In the Huxleyan prophecy, Big Brother does not watch us, by his choice. We watch him, by ours. There is no need for wardens or gates or Ministries of Truth. When a population becomes distracted by trivia, when cultural life is defined as a perpetual round of entertainments, when serious public conversation becomes a form of baby talk, when, in short, people become an audience and their public business a vaudeville act, then a nation finds itself at risk; culture death is a real possibility.
>
> Huxley believed with H. G. Wells that we are in a race between education and disaster, and he wrote continuously about the necessity of our understanding of politics and epistemology of media. In the end, he was trying to tell us that what afflicted the people in Brave New World was not that they were laughing instead of thinking, but that they did not know what they were laughing about and why they had stopped thinking.[10]

Closer to home, it becomes difficult to identify and define cultures, so much so that some say that western backpackers seek culture in other parts of the world because they cannot find it at home. Yet cultures are here. The thinking and rituals around birth, death and marriage are good places to begin. The beginning of life, the end of life and the continuing of life are significant, sacred moments in all cultures. Although there have been phenomenal medical and genetic advances over the last half century, these areas are still ultimately beyond human control. Rituals and ceremonies are means by which human beings manage the mystery and reduce the panic of not being in control. These moments have potential for reconciliation, when people will tell the stories of the past in order to help cope with the present and make decisions about the future. It is often a time when they are open to new perspectives, new stories and narratives, and when they are ready to be transformed. Frequently they may seek to be sustained by spiritual resources that may well be in the form of art. The journalist Andrew Marr, who suffered a severe and disabling stroke in early 2013, said in a radio programme that in his recovery he has been helped and sustained by religious music and poetry, especially the mystical poetry of George Herbert. Marr was surprised to find these helpful, especially as he was not a 'religious' person.[11]

It is in such areas that Christians may join in the work of reconciliation. But to be able to do so churches will need to be aware of the wider cultural movements as well as local variations and personal stories. There will be a discussion of some western cultural trends in the final chapter of this book as it explores reconciling society, but some general points need to be made here. The importance of distinguishing between those cultures that are ephemeral and dehumanizing and those that help people flourish has already been noted. It is also important for Christians to distinguish the parts of culture that can be embraced, those that need to be transformed and those that need to be challenged. To ignore the power and significance of culture and to be dismissive of those parts we find irritating would be a serious error.

Liberation Theology fell into this trap. Born in Latin America in the 1950s and 1960s, it brought an awareness of the structures that oppressed the poor and it influenced thinking across the globe, replicated in different forms in countries beyond Latin America. But one of its weaknesses was that it neglected culture. So while it pointed out the oppressive structures in countries of Latin America, it did not harness the power and resources latent in ancient, indigenous cultures such as the Aztec, Miquito and Mayan. A dialogue between the political and cultural engages the soul of the people which, in turn, touches the depths of the collective human psyche, thereby enabling deeper and more sustainable transformation and change.

The significance of this for our argument is that the Church of England rightly engages with civic society – that is, at the political level – and properly asks the political questions, in particular on behalf of the poor and marginalized. The Church, at its best, is the voice for the poor and for those who have no voice, and it is fulfilling its vocation when using its voice in this way. But if it is to enable the gospel to have a deeper, more profound effect, not just on churchgoers but on society as a whole, it needs to take fuller account of culture. The Church has a good record of ministering to the dying, conducting funeral services and comforting the bereaved. But how much discussion is there about the meaning of death and preparing for death and its cultural implications (a debate whose significance will be developed in Chapter 6)? The Church provides a wonderful environment for marriage, can prepare couples well and conducts splendid wedding ceremonies for both Christians and non-Christians. But there also need to be places of engagement with communities and wider society around the purpose and benefits of marriage in society. Here are cultural issues that emerge from the depths of society, and the way they are handled will define a society's identity. Whether the gospel can touch and transform these depths depends a lot on the Church's willingness to engage at this level. More will be said about the effects of its failure to do so in Chapter 6, but we now examine a very pressing challenge.

Both Church and society are facing significant cultural questions and a potential rift over 'equal' or same-sex marriage. Considering the question from the perspective of culture shines light on particular issues that personal and political perspectives may overlook. Seeing it within the lifetime's quest for reconciliation, which is at the heart of this book, will influence the atmosphere in which conversations about same-sex marriage and, indeed, the whole question of human sexuality will take place. As we have already seen, the quest for reconciliation does not mean that conflict will be avoided, but it does call for a respect for the 'other', who may hold different views, and a realization that because we disagree does not mean we cannot walk together. To be able to disagree with somebody and yet recognize that we share the same faith is a sign of God's love and grace among us. Living with contradictions is one of the marks of reconciliation (see Chapter 3).

Hitherto Church and state have shared similar understandings of marriage, even though they have offered different wedding ceremonies. But with the legalization of same-sex marriage the Church of England's traditional understanding of marriage is now different from that of the state, which regards same-sex marriage as identical to heterosexual marriage.

Many couples – heterosexual and same-sex – wanting to commit themselves to each other do so out of love, and both heterosexual and same-sex couples will share the desire for lifelong companionship. But there are differences between the two forms of relationship that are recognized by cultures across the globe, the most significant of which is expressed in procreation.[12] Culturally there is a difference between a committed same-sex relationship and a committed heterosexual relationship. Not all heterosexual married couples have children. This does not make a marriage any less a marriage, but when a male and female come together they have the potential to become parents through procreation because of their sexual complementarity, and this is reflected in the Christian marriage service when it describes marriage as a gift of God in creation.[13] Therefore it is difficult to see how marriage, as the Church understands it, can reflect the reality of a partnership into which a same-sex couple may wish to enter.[14] For these reasons, ideally a different form of civil union needs to be constructed that reflects the relationship into which the same-sex couple will enter. The Church cannot accept the idea of marriage between a same-sex couple; how will it relate to a different form of covenanted relationship?

Such questions will be in the background of the 'facilitated conversations' recommended by the working party set up by the House of Bishops and chaired by Sir Joseph Pilling.[15] The conversations are to focus on the 'subject of sexuality with its history of deeply entrenched views', and will take place not just within the Church of England but ecumenically and across the whole of the Anglican Communion, and will be set primarily within the context of human flourishing.[16] This is a vast undertaking and will require the grace of God and the love and patience of the whole Christian community with its wide spectrum of views on sexuality and same-sex marriage. The conversations will require a safe environment in which it will be possible to listen in a non-judging way to the stories and experiences of others. They will require forgiveness and refusing the role of victimhood, and a willingness on the part of all parties to have their views challenged and changed. Celebration and thanksgiving will also need to be part of the conversations. There will be many challenges in embracing great diversity. In some parts of the world, being seen as a place of welcome and acceptance to gay people can risk the lives of vulnerable people within the Church; in others, not being seen that way is akin to the rejection of Christ himself.

There is a danger that loud voices speaking in terms of rights and politics polarize the questions and determine the theological shape of the debate. Among the questions reconciliation raises is that of otherness, respecting difference, and that is something singularly lacking here. The differences between same-sex relationships and heterosexual marriages are to be celebrated and respected rather than feared. Conducting the conversations within the common quest for reconciliation has the potential to change the atmosphere in which the debate takes place, locating it in the context of gift and mission. In essence the framework of reconciliation will, it is hoped, provide a new language and a new way in which to discuss these weighty matters.

Marriage is regarded as a gift of God in creation and has a missionary potential in what it says to society about God, love and commitment. One of the questions the Church will need to address in relation to committed partnerships between same-sex couples is whether they too are regarded as gifts of God in what they say to society about God, love and commitment.

At the same time, being reminded that it is reconciliation to God and not reconciliation to society that is being sought will go a long way to ensure that the Church will only accommodate the norms of society if, after prayer and deliberation, it discerns that God is speaking through them.

Relationships

In Chapter 3, relationship is described as the cornerstone of reconciliation. Jesus Christ, the embodiment of reconciliation, is also the embodiment of God's love and relationship with the world. The Church, which is the body of Christ, is therefore called to embody reconciliation and God's love.

In any institution (including the Church), relationships are managed and mediated through structures that should reflect and communicate the values of the institution. The structures should be the servant of the institution and if they become its master then there needs to be a reassessment of priorities. Structures that are not well constructed or, more perniciously, outmoded, can draw out and parade the negative – which lies within every person and institution – and show the power of intransigence instead of the potential of transformation. Such was the struggle Paul faced with the Church in Corinth where, when they were together, they allowed their socio-economic and cultural divisions, which characterized the society in which they lived, to dominate their oneness in Christ and the running of the Christian community. This was a hindrance to the Corinthian Church being a reconciling church. Paul used the image of the body as a model for the different groupings to relate.

It is becoming increasingly clear that, for similar reasons, the governance – in particular the synodical system – within the Church of England, organized and administered by good, dedicated and saintly people, needs radical revision because it obscures some of the key values for which the Church stands.[17] The socio-economic and cultural climate in which the synodical system was constructed over 40 years ago has radically changed. General Synod, the Church's national assembly, along with diocesan and deanery synods, may reflect the Church of the present and certainly of the past, but definitely not the Church of the future.

The fortieth anniversary of synodical government was marked in 2010 – there was much for which to be thankful. The synodical system firmly established the voice of laity within the governance of the Church and has provided a dynamic where laity, clergy and bishops can meet to order and manage the institution. However, the present system, a child of the twentieth century, is no longer fit for purpose in the twenty-first. In recent elections, dioceses have found it difficult to encourage people to commit themselves to deanery as well as diocesan synods. Many people whose talents and insights would be valuable in these bodies simply do not put themselves forward for election. Deanery synods, in particular, are frequently regarded as bodies in search of reasons to meet. In addition, when General Synod meets only on weekdays, usually taking five days at a time, at least twice or sometimes three times a year, how representative can its membership be? There are not many groups of laypeople who could or would wish to be available to take nine or ten days from their holiday allowance to attend meetings. It follows that the various synods are not regarded as either representative or relevant to the activities of the wider Church.

A number of reasons lie behind this deteriorating confidence in the synodical system, but here are two. First, the western, parliamentary, adversarial culture on which the synodical system is based does not provide a creative environment for debate and decision making for the people of God. The debating style is such that the argument is won when the opposing argument is crushed: while it is important to have a vigorous debate, the 'wisdom of the quiet' is not taken into account. Some may flourish in such an environment; others wilt. Second, the bureaucratic systems developed to support the structure are now tending to dominate it. This leads to a materialistic fatalism, where the cycle of cause and effect trundles on without challenge. Measuring performance, benchmarking and agreed outcomes (significant as they are) elbow out imagination and risk (important as they are). The outcome is that the Church as a whole devotes an increasing amount of its energy resources to defensive bureaucratic systems whose task is to protect it if challenged, and thereby devotes a decreasing amount of energy on promoting the good news of Jesus Christ.

The Church necessarily needs to be *synodal*, so that those who have the responsibility to lead and manage can consult with the whole body of believers, but it does not necessarily need to be *synodical*. Synodal means walking the way together. For Anglicans, being synodal indicates the way laity, clergy and bishops are held together – in synod – as they do this. The Anglican–Roman Catholic document entitled *The Gifts of Authority* points out that being synodal expresses our vocation as people of the way (Acts 9.2) to live, work and journey together in Christ who is the way (John 14.6).[18]

One of the blessings of belonging to a worldwide Church is that one part of it can learn from the experience of others. There are some communities that focus on the need for consensus before decisions are made. For example, the World Council of Churches (WCC) has adopted a method of coming to its decisions by consensus. This may prove a lengthy process but it does mean that it is not only those with the confidence to intervene whose voices will be taken into account. The wisdom of the quiet can also be heard. This method of decision making has enabled churches to remain within the WCC who may otherwise have left.

Every ten years the Lambeth Conference draws together bishops from across the Anglican Communion. The 2008 Conference moved away from the adversarial process of debate by meeting in indaba groups. The indaba process has its origins in South Africa and creates an environment where listening is valued above speaking. It does not prevent disagreement but provides a place where difference can be respected. Following the 2008 Lambeth Conference a 'continuing indaba' process has been set up whose aim is to: 'enable Anglicans worldwide to live reconciliation by facing our own conflicts, celebrate our diversity and difference and so become agents of reconciliation in the world'.

Archbishop Paul Kwong from Hong Kong said this of the indaba:

> The indaba process encourages genuine conversation across differences. It seeks to build trust and models a way of decision-making that is not confrontational or 'parliamentary', rather it emphasises mutual and intense listening to deeply held opinions and a willingness to dig deeper in order to find the shared values that lie at the root of our common faith.[19]

Protestant churches in Germany have utilized the *Kirchentag*, a form of biennial church congress that draws people – young and old – in their thousands to engage with theological, social and political themes through worship, discussion and drama.

Today's culture of shrill voices and polarized opinions is different from that of 40 years ago, when the parliamentary model may have been right for the synod of the people of God. I believe this is no longer the case. This is not a path towards reconciliation but towards polarization. The future is open to debate, but one possibility is to include the *Kirchentag* element in a synodal system in which there could be regular, but occasional, large and inspiring gatherings where issues in theology can be aired through a variety of media, including drama, debate and liturgy. A system for today is required. Nothing will be perfect, but there is need for a vehicle that is in touch with the energy of the Holy Spirit, the aspirations of the people of God and the realities of the world.

A reconciling church will be open to building relationships with outside bodies if by doing so reconciliation is enabled. Chapter 6 will look at the relationship between the Church and society; here we consider its relationship with other faith communities, both Christian and other.

If a church is the only faith community in a village and there is no other Christian community with which it can realistically relate, it is the willingness and openness to relate to others that is important. Even if a church is in a community that is far away from other faiths such as Islam, Hinduism and Sikhism, it is the willingness and openness to be in dialogue with the beliefs and world views of other faiths that is key. The questions posed by other faith traditions are important for the whole country and not just for the communities where they are located. The smallest and remotest community in the UK will be affected by the fact that we are living and working on a world stage. We need only switch on our TVs, open our newspapers, see where our clothes are made and note where our vegetables are grown to be aware of that. Similarly, the brutal killing of an off-duty soldier in a suburb of London by men claiming to be avenging the death of Muslims killed by British armed forces reverberates through the remotest parts of the country as well as the area in which the killing took place. A reconciling church will want to be open to dialogue with other faiths to understand what is happening and discover how it can work for reconciliation. In the community of Woolwich, where the killing took place, Christians and Muslims have been working together, condemning the action and determining ways of cooperation that will deter, as far as possible, similar events from happening.[20]

A reconciling church will also want to be in relationship with other Christian traditions. Close to the shore of Lake Geneva, about 15 miles north-east of Geneva itself, the Château de Bossey houses the Ecumenical Institute of the World Council of Churches. Bossey – as the institute is known – was founded by a General Secretary of the World Council of Churches in 1946, when its inaugural lecture by its first director prophetically marked the pioneering path Bossey was to take. The title of the lecture was 'The Christian Church in a World of Crisis'. For more than six decades Bossey has held annual graduate schools and courses whose students – lay and ordained – reflect the rich tapestry of Christian denominations and cultures from around the world. It has in effect been shaping future leaders of the Church through worship, learning and encounter. Attending the graduate school will be Africans, Asians, Australasians, Americans and Europeans, who may be Pentecostal, Methodist, Orthodox, Anglican, Reformed, Lutheran, Baptist, Congregational, Roman Catholic and Presbyterian, among others. Over their four-month stay they live, eat, pray and study together. They learn an enormous amount about reconciliation as they tell their stories and listen to others'. Stories of oppression and hunger, war and refugees, poverty and wealth live side by side. The relationship between gospel and culture and the role of Church unity are not just discussed but lived in an intercultural environment where laughter and tears mingle with joy and pain. Bossey has touched the lives of many of its students, who discover that working and praying for Christian unity is not primarily in order to reorganize Christ's Church, rather to transform Christ's world. Dr Ioan Sauca, an orthodox priest from Romania and the present director, writes of Bossey in these terms:

> The tremendous social fractures which we are witnessing worldwide, and the accelerated transformations in the Christian world, mean that such a uniquely diverse centre of encounter and learning has rarely before been so necessary. The churches, and the world, still need a Bossey.[21]

Just as relating to other faiths needs to be seen against the backdrop of the world stage, so too does relating to other Christian communities. It is more than a pooling of resources. Fellowship with other churches is important for the sake of mission. Jesus' prayer for unity in St John's Gospel is so that 'the world may believe that you have sent me' (John 17.21). The shape and organization of the fellowship may vary according to local contexts but the goal of these reconciling Christian communities is for mission.

In the UK there is currently a mixed picture in ecumenical relations. While there appears little institutional appetite for unity there is some local energy. In places, councils of churches are collaborating on projects ranging from shared study courses to organizing the increasing number of food banks across the country. There is at least one example of a group of churches from different denominations sponsoring an ecumenical, secondary 'free school'. Another development in ecumenical relations is a fuller involvement of newer Christian communities, such as community churches and new-generation churches. As each newer Christian community tends to be independent, caution is required in making generalizations about the way they operate, but for some, the former suspicion between them and traditional churches that hampered cooperation is disappearing.

There are signs of a different form of ecumenism emerging. A new vision for Christian unity – a new form of reconciling – needs to be articulated that will take account of theological, social and political realities. It need not be too complicated – perhaps a starting point would be the call to worship together to serve the poor. The world stage on which the churches are operating will ideally be brought into the local story. Institutions like Bossey demonstrate how this can be done. Jesus' prayer for unity, that his followers may be one so that the world may believe, is a call for reconciliation.

Authority

The struggle of authority is as much an issue today as it was for St Paul. In the Church in Corinth those who questioned Paul's authority said they were followers of Cephas (Peter), Apollos or Christ. On a number of occasions he had to convince his hearers that he had a good, Jewish pedigree, but what comes across clearly in Scripture is that the ultimate authority for a Christian leader is located in following the example of Jesus Christ, who was willing to suffer and die not just for his followers but for his enemies, even those who killed him. This is reconciliation at its sharpest. It was through his wounds that Jesus' disciples recognized him. Paul picks this theme up in his second letter to the Corinthians:

> We are afflicted in every way, but not crushed; perplexed, but not driven to despair; persecuted, but not forsaken; struck down, but not destroyed; always carrying in the body the death of Jesus, so that the life of Jesus may also be made visible in our bodies. For while we live, we are always being given up to death for Jesus' sake, so that the life of Jesus may be made visible in our mortal flesh. So death is at work in us, but life in you.
>
> (2 Cor. 4.8–12)

Authority is bound up with power and vulnerability, which is one of the marks of reconciliation.

The UK in the twenty-first century is facing crises of authority. Institutions previously viewed as trustworthy and regarded as icons of authority – the police, Parliament, the press and even the Church – are no longer viewed that way.

The Church too has its own crises of authority. There are powerful interest groups within it who say they would leave if certain lines were crossed. Decisions around the ordination of women (to the priesthood and to be bishops) have seen a number leave the Church (often to join another), because although it has declared that such changes are consonant with the faith, they disagree and find it impossible to remain. There are other faithful Anglicans who also find it difficult to accept the ordination of women but do remain because the Church of England is their home and family. Being in this position cannot be easy but it is a reminder that reconciliation involves living with difference.

The different ways of interpreting and understanding Scripture, which have become particularly apparent in recent debates around sexuality, have provoked a great deal of disagreement.[22] As a result, some churches have left the fellowship or diocese while others have remained but distanced themselves or expressed protest by withholding or reducing financial contributions towards central costs.

Similar disputes have afflicted churches worldwide. In the USA a number of churches have broken away from the main Anglican Church – the Episcopal Church – because of the tendency towards 'liberalism' and the way the Bible is interpreted. They have formed the Anglican Church in North America, which has its own bishops and constitution.

Another ecclesiological fault line has appeared in the Anglican Church with the formation of Gafcon (Global Anglican Future Conference) in 2008. Gafcon consists of a number of dioceses in Africa who began to journey together when they believed that traditional Christian morality was being compromised (again over issues of sexuality), that there was doctrinal error and that biblical truth was being abandoned in the way texts were interpreted. A close link – cemented by a grouping called Fellowship of Confessing Anglicans – was formed between some churches in the UK and Gafcon churches because of shared theological concerns. The Gafcon movement remains within the Anglican Communion but there have been strained relationships, which were apparent when many of the dioceses represented by their bishops at the first Gafcon Conference in 2008 in Jerusalem were not represented at the Lambeth Conference in 2008. Reconciliation calls on all parties involved to be open to transformation in negotiations such as these.

St Paul would have been familiar with the divisions and disputes being faced by the Church today and would undoubtedly say that Christian communities that are not reconciled among themselves are not reconciled to God, even though God may be reconciled to them. Being reconciled to each other does not mean believing in the same way but it does mean being in relationship and recognizing God at work in the other, even though the one may not agree with the other. Living with contradictions, being able to hold together when confronted with two apparently contradictory truths, has been part of the identity of the Church throughout its history, and being able to do so sends an important message to wider society about truth and unity (see Chapter 3). Again, what makes reconciliation possible is not whether one party agrees with another but the way disagreement is handled.

New reconciling communities

One of the means of recognizing the seriousness with which a church takes reconciliation is through its growing and encouragement of other communities of reconciliation. Another word that could be used for this is mission. Speaking of mission in terms of the founding of other reconciling communities sharpens the focus of a word that is used so frequently and imprecisely that its meaning is lost.

Ray and Violet Sinden, with the support of their five daughters and two sons, ran a successful and prosperous farm near Sevenoaks in Kent. Violet always had a strong Christian faith; Ray, although brought up in a Christian household, had not practised his faith for many years until he was drawn back into church in 1965 at the age of 48.

Olive, Ray's and Violet's eldest daughter, was a friend of a Church Army captain called Paul Deeming, who worked among the homeless on the streets of East London. Paul invited Ray to join him in his work one evening. Ray went grudgingly, thinking that their trying to help was a waste of time. But this turned out to be a time of deep transformation for Ray, who was able to see the person beyond the problems homelessness brought. As a result, and driven by his personal experience of God's love, Ray wanted to show others that there was a God who loved them. Ray met a number of homeless people who, although they were sober and had turned their back on drink, were fearful they would return to their old habits because they had no place to stay and no future prospects. Life looked grim. Ray decided to take some of these men back home for rehabilitation. They were offered a large flat over a garage block and they joined the family in the farmhouse for meals, Bible study and leisure.

Their first guest, a Canadian war pensioner, came in June 1967. He was able to pay a small amount towards his keep and did some work in the garden. He stayed with the family for a year and was soon joined by three others.

The farm eventually became overcrowded. At this time Ray had been touched by the same verse from St Matthew's Gospel that had touched Antony of Egypt: 'If you wish to be perfect, go, sell your possessions, and give the money to the poor, and you will have treasure in heaven; then come, follow me.' (Matt. 19.21).

Like Antony, Ray took Jesus' instruction literally: he sold the farm to buy a much larger house to accommodate a greater number of homeless people. In 1968 Ray and Violet moved into a 37-room mansion in need of renovation, situated in a 15-acre country estate. The house, near Maidstone, was called Kenward and the move marked the beginning of the Kenward Trust. Nearly 40 years on, the Trust accommodates around 200 residents across eight buildings each year. In addition it reaches hundreds of young people through prevention initiatives and helps others with advice and support. Kenward also provides vocational and resettlement opportunities for offenders from local prisons, and support for families affected by addiction.

The aim of the Trust remains as it has always been, namely to break through alcohol and drug addiction and dependency, thereby making it possible for people to choose to lead new and productive lives. All this happens in an unashamed Christian environment, though recovery and support programmes are not religion-based. People from all backgrounds and faiths are welcomed. Those who work for the Trust believe in people when they no longer believe in themselves. Its strapline is 'Transforming lives, creating choice'. Kenward is a reconciling community founded by a couple who had experienced transformation and reconciliation in their lives.[23]

A reconciling church calls for reconciling worship

Anglicans in Harare, Zimbabwe, faced difficult years from 2008 until 2012 when they were forced from their church buildings and properties by a previous bishop, Nolbert Kunonga, because they refused to leave the Anglican Church in Central Africa to form a new Church of which he would be the head. His actions were supported by the state police, who threatened, teargassed, beat, arrested and imprisoned many who questioned what was happening. Anglicans were not violent in their response and took every opportunity to negotiate and enter into dialogue with the police and those in power. Without their buildings they had to worship in marquees, borrowed premises and under trees. There were occasions when Anglicans from across Harare worshipped together in its central Africa Unity Square. Each time the joy and thankfulness within the worship could not be quashed or subdued by the fear of beatings or teargas.

Over this period, when Anglicans were exiled from their own buildings, many others joined the Church when they saw the way worshippers were witnessing to their faith. A number of police, so moved by their attitude, also decided to worship with them. The numbers grew so much that there were concerns that when worshippers were allowed back into their own churches, some of the buildings would now be too small.[24] Reconciling worship mediated through the attitude of forgiveness, reconciliation, joy and openness, and all displayed though worship, attracted many followers. Through conflict and vulnerability they were a people whose reconciling worship encouraged and attracted others.

Worship is at the heart of the life of a church, and unless its worship is reconciling, attractive to others, it cannot be a reconciling church. The Eucharist is the sacrament of reconciliation but there is a variety of forms of worship. So what does reconciling worship look like?

The five 'drivers' in Chapter 2 and the 15 'marks' of reconciliation in Chapter 3 can be used as a checklist to explore the extent that worship is reconciling. For example, is worship a source of new energy, life and hope? Is relationship – with God, each other and the world – a cornerstone of the church? How far is it possible to listen in worship? Are stories – of God and of people – narrated in worship? How are conflict and contradictions handled in worship? Is otherness – of God and people – acknowledged and respected in worship?

Africa Unity Square in Harare is the perfect setting for worship. In the heart of the city it is close to the shopping area and adjacent to the Zimbabwean Parliament building. The liberating message of joy in the heat of struggle and transformation in the middle of commerce and politics speak powerfully about reconciling with God.

For individual, quiet reflection

1 Consider the social mix in your own church community. Which aspects of the church's life, work and worship are both strengthened and hampered by the variety?
2 What has made you feel welcomed, or not, when you have visited other church communities, perhaps when holidaying at home or abroad? If you have been warmly received, would that be sufficient to encourage you to return, especially if the tradition of that congregation differed substantially from your own?

3 What attracts you about the worship of your own congregation, and which features of that worship – praise, joy, penitence, thanksgiving – do you find most reconciling?

For discussion in groups

1 The opening sentence of this chapter offers a vision of the Church's vocation. What is your assessment of the Church's role in today's world, and is this role constant or one that changes with the generations?
2 Are St Paul's insights into, and concerns about, the Christian community in Corinth similar to those we face today? What lessons can be learnt from his injunctions to the Christians in Corinth?
3 Should changes be made to the decision-making structures of the Church to enable both participation and decision making to be brought nearer to those who make up 'the body of Christ' in local congregations? Where does real leadership lie in your experience of the Church – and how do you think your own voice can be more effectively heard?
4 What are the potentially divisive issues in your church? How can they most fruitfully be discussed?

Prayer

Eternal God, unchanging, reaching out and drawing in, encompassing all that you have made in arms of love, forgive our lack of love, our selfishness, our reliance on ourselves, and our prejudices and discriminations in a world that you have designed to be in harmony; grant us generosity of word, thought and action, the assurance of your love and forgiveness when we fail and fall, and the peace that comes from knowing that you are with us always and everywhere. Give us the insight to know that what seems beyond our grasp and comprehension will show itself to be that which loves, abides, and clings for ever, the self-giving of your Son, our Saviour Jesus Christ. Amen.

Derek Carpenter

6

A reconciling society

Pedro Reyes, a Mexican sculptor, has taken thousands of guns and transformed them into musical instruments. Handguns are made into violins, rifles into a rustic piano and gun barrels welded together to make pan pipes. Reyes has constructed a fully mechanized orchestra. The weapons, seized by the army in the war against drug cartels, have wrecked thousands of lives in northern Mexico, where the murder rate is phenomenally high. Reyes believed that a kind of exorcism was taking place when his instruments were played – that the music chased away the demons these weapons held and served as a requiem for the people killed.

Pedro Reyes' work and words are powerful stories of reconciliation. He also shows the role music can play in reconciliation, something that will become more apparent in this chapter. Reyes transforms the weapons that had killed and brought fear into instruments that soothe and bring peace. The weapons contained memories of past pain and death but were transformed into instruments of life and hope; they trapped and controlled in this world but became instruments that liberated and released into others. The world's societies are packed with similar stories and filled with the potential for reconciliation, some of which this chapter will relate. But alongside stories of reconciliation are other, darker stories.

Reyes' work is a reminder that reconciliation is not just a longing and aspiration for people of faith – it is a cry at the heart of the whole of creation.[1] Human beings flourish when they are reconciled with God, within themselves, between themselves – societies and nations – and with creation. This book has argued that it is not possible to achieve such reconciliation in this life but that it is possible to shape this life as a journey to Reconciliation (big 'R'), enjoying experiences of reconciliation (small 'r') on the journey (see Chapter 3, p. 45). Using the drivers and marks of reconciliation identified in Chapters 2 and 3, this chapter explores to what extent we live in a society that encourages and supports reconciliation. Does our society provide fertile ground for reconciliation to grow and flourish? How can the Church encourage society to be more open to reconciliation?

It is in the being of the Church that it needs constantly to be reformed and transformed; so too is it in the being of society. Today's opportunities and challenges cannot be met by a society constructed to handle yesterday's – that would be akin to fighting the First World War with the weaponry used 100 years earlier at the Battle of Waterloo. Society is an even more complex body than the Church. Consisting of a wide array of social groupings of all faiths and none, and driven by an even wider range of cultures, British society is subject to a common and dispersed political authority sharing a generally agreed – though disputed by some – geographical area. Although there is great diversity there are some common trends that are shared, not just within the UK but further afield. The world is now a global family, sometimes at war with itself, and so stories, examples and illustrations will be drawn from around the world. 'Society' here can mean any society, but towards the end there will be a focus on issues faced by British society, many of which will be recognizable to people who live in other so-called western societies.

First we look at examples of reconciliation, then at signs of enmity – the opposite of reconciliation. We then acknowledge that just as there is within humanity the potential for reconciliation, so too is there the potential for destruction. Finally, after considering some recent cultural trends within British society, we suggest some ways the Church can respond to help society be more open to the possibilities of reconciliation.

Signs of reconciliation

Truth and reconciliation commissions

If a person is asked which country has had a truth and reconciliation commission, the answer will probably be South Africa. The South Africa Truth and Reconciliation Commission was a significant body charged with a task that was to make a statement beyond South Africa. The Commission, chaired by Archbishop Desmond Tutu, was established in 1995 with the brief to bear witness to, record and where appropriate grant amnesty to the perpetrators of crimes relating to human rights violations. It could also recommend reparation and rehabilitation. A great deal of time was spent hearing people's stories. It was generally thought that the Commission was more effective in getting the truth than achieving reconciliation, but its very existence was symbolic, making a powerful statement about the importance of truth and reconciliation and enabling people to lament over what happened in the past.

But there have been many other truth and reconciliation commissions. A National Truth and Reconciliation Commission was established in Chile to investigate deaths and disappearances under General Pinochet's rule. A report was released in 1991. The Liberian Truth and Reconciliation Commission was established in 2005 to promote national peace, security, unity and reconciliation after more than 20 years of civil conflict. A Truth and Reconciliation Commission was set up in the Solomon Islands in the light of the ethnic violence that gripped the country between 1997 and 2003. Its purpose was to address people's traumatic experiences and promote national unity and reconciliation.[2] In 1999 the Sierra Leone Truth and Reconciliation Commission was set up in the wake of an 11-year civil war to record civil rights violations and abuses, respond to the needs of those who suffered, promote healing and reconciliation and prevent a repetition of the violations and abuses suffered. The effectiveness of these commissions has been mixed but their very establishment is a sign of the countries' concern to bring about peaceful coexistence at the very least.

Closer to home we have the Consultative Group on the Past in Northern Ireland, jointly chaired by Archbishop Robin Eames and Denis Bradley. As already stated, it was set up to consult across the community on how Northern Ireland can best approach the legacy of the events of the past 40 years and recommend steps to help build a shared future not dominated by events of the past. Its report was not without its challenges and was finally published in 2009. Among its recommendations were the recognition of the importance of storytelling as a basis for reconciliation and of healing through remembering. But of most significance was its reflection that whether or not any of its 31 recommendations were implemented, the report provides an opportunity to reflect on Northern Ireland's progress towards reconciliation, the remaining tensions in Northern Ireland and the work that remains to be done. Again, the importance of such an exercise is not whether the objectives are achieved, rather that it provides space and opportunity to step back and reflect on what stage has been reached along the road to reconciliation.

These are reminders that the longing and aspiration towards reconciliation lie deep in the heart of humanity; that when people tire of fighting, these seek expression. The Christian faith, with its engagement with reconciliation for more than 2,000 years (though not always to good effect), is well placed to engage actively in wider society on matters of reconciliation, not just as a means of conflict resolution but as a way of shaping society. It is worth noting that the expertise of people of faith is sometimes recognized by the civic authorities – for example, Anglican archbishops chaired the South African Truth and Reconciliation Commission and the Consultative Group on the Past in Northern Ireland, while a Methodist Bishop chaired the Sierra Leone Truth and Reconciliation Commission.

The Singing Revolution

We have already seen in Chapter 3 that the longing and aspiration towards reconciliation can lead to conflict. It can also lead to revolution, especially when its expression rises up from within. The 'Singing Revolution' that led to the liberation of the Baltic state of Estonia is a good example of reconciliation flourishing and deepening in a climate of celebration and thanksgiving. Once the citizens of Estonia had, literally, found their voice, liberation quickly followed. From 1939 to 1991 Estonia was under the iron grip first of Germany – until 1944 – and then the Soviet Union, when it annexed the Baltic States. Although Estonia formally gained independence in 1991, the last of the Soviet troops did not leave until 1994. Under Soviet occupation many Estonians were taken to Siberia and never heard of again. Even today major churches in some towns have a box of Siberian earth to memorialize the many who disappeared. Another reminder of this harsh period is the symbol of the broken cornflower. Representation of the cornflower, the national flower of Estonia, was banned; the broken cornflower, alongside Siberian earth, hint at the trauma of these long years of occupation.

Another way that the Soviets tried to break the spirit of Estonia was by the banning of Estonian songs and hymns. Estonia found this ban particularly hard as singing was a form of national expression: since 1869 the country had been holding national song festivals every five years. Since Estonian national identity was fed and deepened through song, the ban was an attack on the soul of the country. In the latter part of the 1980s the Soviet Union began to unravel, but Moscow hoped that the Baltic States would, with some relaxation of restrictions such as on freedom of speech, remain in the USSR. This was not the wish of Estonians. From 1987 Estonians gathered in public places to sing songs that were strictly forbidden. In May 1988 there was a pop festival in the second city of Estonia (Tartu), where five patriotic songs were sung. Doing this so publicly was particularly symbolic because Tartu is home to a huge Soviet air base built to launch attacks against the West. Four months later, in the capital Tallinn, a massive song festival was held that drew nearly 300,000 people – more than a quarter of all Estonians. By this time political leaders were actively participating, formally demanding independence. The Singing Revolution, helping towards a form of inner reconciliation, gave Estonians the confidence and self-belief that the push for independence needed. Although political reconciliation cannot be achieved while the struggle is raging, but is only possible when parties regarding themselves as equal sit down to negotiate, inner reconciliation provides the oppressed or victimized with the self-confidence to work towards political and social equilibrium that may then lead to reconciliation. In this way reconciliation leads to conflict, which in its turn is the pathway to reconciliation.

Reconciliation arising from tragedy

There are moving examples of reconciliation in local communities, sometimes arising out of tragedy. Rob Knox was an 18-year-old rising actor who played the part of Marcus Belby alongside Daniel Radcliffe in *Harry Potter and the Half-Blood Prince*. Less than six months before the film was released in November 2008, Rob was stabbed to death in Sidcup, south-east London, after his younger brother had been threatened by a man wielding knives. Rob, a sports lover, was a member of the same rugby club as Jimmy Mizen, a 16-year-old who had been fatally stabbed two weeks before in nearby Lee. Jimmy, a much-loved brother and son, was also with his brother when his jugular vein was severed by somebody threatening his brother.

Losing young people full of promise and potential was devastating, especially for their families. But the response of the parents was remarkable. Both sets of parents set up foundations in memory of their sons. Both were established to promote the good in young people and to draw out their potential. The community has been mobilized in support of these aims.[3] In addition a Peace Cup tournament was set up in memory of both Rob Knox and Jimmy Mizen. The annual five-a-side football tournament is played by boys and girls from Sidcup-based primary schools who are in year six (ten and eleven years old), and its aim is to promote peace through sport. The tournament is unusual in that points are awarded for good sportsmanship and removed for bad. The Peace Cup, like the foundations, is aiming to create a safe environment where the best in young people is encouraged.

There are other examples across the globe where the most dreadful circumstances have elicited such heroism. The human spirit can soar to great heights against all the odds, with the result that possibilities are created that enable others to do the same. Victimhood is shunned, good comes out of evil and a reconciling society is given energy and encouragement. The early Christian theologian Tertullian said that the blood of the martyrs is the seed of the Church; in a similar way, through the actions of courageous people able to dig deep into their God-given humanity, great tragedy can elicit noble responses that form a strong basis for a reconciling society.

The environment

Another sign of reconciliation in society is seen in worldwide environmental awareness. This is an area where interpretations are contested, but it has been conclusively established and widely accepted that the resources of the planet will be exhausted unless humanity changes its attitude towards creation and the environment. From recycling schemes to solar panels, from concerns about the melting of the polar ice cap to overfishing, societies across the world are alert to issues surrounding the sustaining of the planet. Having fallen out of relationship with creation and having for millennia seen the planet as a resource to be used and exploited, there are signs that societies and individuals are trying to reconcile themselves to the wonderful resources entrusted to us. Societies attempt this by national and international schemes and treaties, and individuals work towards reconciliation by using creative methods.

Chapter 4 began with mention of Joel Salatin's concept of 'Forgiveness Farming'. Salatin, who farms in the Shenandoah Valley in Virginia in the USA, is a third-generation alternative farmer and has himself farmed full-time since 1982. Examining Forgiveness Farming in greater detail reveals the extent to which the drivers and marks of reconciliation are part of the thinking behind it. There are ten key components: relationship forgiveness; emotional forgiveness; infrastructure forgiveness; landscape forgiveness; health forgiveness; weather forgiveness; price forgiveness; marketing forgiveness; product forgiveness; neighbour forgiveness. Here is some detail of four in this list.

First there is relationship forgiveness, which refers to relationships with and between those working on the farm. Without a common mission statement towards which everybody in the team feels comfortable in contributing, there cannot be a thriving farm. The well-being of every member of the team needs to be taken into account. Second, there is emotional forgiveness, where the farmer has a healthy and sustainable relationship with the environment and with the animals. The farmer needs to regard him- or herself as 'nature's nurturer' rather than 'nature's conqueror', respecting and honouring creation for what it is. This draws in the theme of otherness – colourfully demonstrated when Salatin writes of the need to honour the 'pigness of the pig'. Third, there is infrastructure forgiveness, where farmers are encouraged not to put all their eggs in one infrastructure basket. Investing heavily in one form of farming, thereby effectively making the farm single-use, enslaves the farmer and future generations to the past. Trends and economic needs change – there needs to be versatility so that the infrastructure can be adapted in response. Finally there is neighbour forgiveness. There is a need to be aware of and to listen to the neighbour. Salatin is saddened by the ways farms have alienated neighbours – some of whom are new to the countryside – with unsightly structures and putrid smells. He argues that farming operations need to be aesthetically pleasant and the animals content. The alienation of neighbours is symbolic of the 'anti-human industrial food system that divorces food courtship from dinner and turns the populace into farm-haters' which, comments Salatin, 'is a tragedy of epic proportions'.[4] Whatever one's attitude to organic farming and eco-agriculture, undoubtedly the thinking and philosophy, seeking a new relationship with the environment, are couched in terms of reconciliation. Forgiveness, otherness, new energy, relationship, listening, narrative, hope, power and vulnerability are characteristics of Forgiveness Farming.

Again there is a darker side because despite some impressive advances in environmental concern, we seem to have encountered a brick wall. World leaders have signed over 500 agreements on the environment and climate change over the last half century. Most have come to nothing. Countries sign agreements at international conferences that too often do not pass into domestic law. There has been 'treaty congestion'. Furthermore with the world financial crisis the environment has been dropping lower down the political agenda. The environment was not a topic discussed in the public debates between the two candidates for the US presidential election in 2012, and it is receding from the political agenda in the UK. There is regional energy and commitment to the environmental agenda but it is lacking on the national and international stages. The gravity and urgency of the challenge has not been grasped amid so many other matters vying for attention. It may be regarded as an important cause, even life and death for the planet, but in difficult times it is treated as an expendable luxury.

And there is evidence that our understanding of what is happening to the planet is more limited than we think. There has been some indication that global warming has been slowing, which some have viewed as the result of greater care exercised towards the environment. However, scientists point out that what appears to be an improvement is due to natural cycles that bring fluctuation within the climate – the general outlook is still bleak.[5] We may be more aware of the environmental challenges ahead but we are far from having formed the right relationship with creation to face them.

Signs of enmity

Enmity is the opposite of reconciliation. In the story of the fall, the book of Genesis relates that the serpent persuaded Eve to tempt Adam to eat the fruit God had forbidden them to eat. 'Enmity' is the word frequently used to describe the relationship of distrust and fear that developed between the serpent and humanity as a result of what happened (Gen. 3.15). Whereas one needs to search for signs of reconciliation in society, signs of enmity abound. Here is where the darker stories are to be found. Pick up any newspaper, listen to any news channel and they will be dominated by war, breakdown, negativity, greed and political intrigue. News of reconciliation, grudgingly related, will be carefully examined to discover potential holes and pitfalls. Too often the real stories of reconciliation are to be found in the obituaries.

Just as the potential for good and the potential for evil lie in every human being, so too do they for every society. As a result of a helicopter crashing into the busy Clutha Pub in Glasgow on 29 November 2013, ten people died and 32 were injured. There were stories of heroism as people from the street, without thinking of their own safety, rushed into the badly damaged building to help rescue the injured. On the other hand, the harsh financial climate that has been a feature of many societies since 2008 has seen the demonization of vulnerable groups within society – for example, there have been incidences of disabled people being shouted at and jostled in the street. In addition, the concerns about security that have haunted society since 9/11 have polarized ethnic differences in some communities and brought tension to them. While people do have a choice in the way they react to what happens around and to them, there is no doubt, as we have seen, that some circumstances bring out the best in them while others bring out the worst.

There is the potential for both peacemaking and violence within every human being. The same energy can be used for the common good or for negative and destructive purposes. It can be used for enmity or reconciliation. While we can each decide how we will deploy this energy, it can be touched when we least expect. Furthermore we can surprise ourselves by our reaction, which may be shaped by a variety of influences, including society and those around us. The saintly Jean Vanier, founder of the L'Arche communities, describes the violence within him when confronted with the penetrating screaming of Lucien, a mentally disabled young man:

> The pitch of Lucien's scream was piercing
> and seemed to penetrate the very core of my being,
> awakening my own inner anguish.
> I could sense anger, violence, and even hatred
> rising up within me.
> I would have been capable of hurting him to keep him quiet.
> It was as if a part of my being that I had learned to control
> was exploding.
> It was not only Lucien's anguish
> that was difficult for me to accept
> but the revelation of what was in my own heart,
> – my capacity to hurt others –
> I who have been called to share my life with the weak,
> had a power of hatred for a weak person! . . .
> How painful it is for us to look reality in the face,
> to discover our own fragility
> and our capacity for anger and hatred.[6]

Society, made up of a mixture of human beings influenced and shaped by what goes on both inside and outside of them, by what has happened in the past and to what they aspire in the future, has the capacity for good and evil, for reconciliation and enmity.

When will they ever learn?

In 2010 the *New Statesman* listed the folksong 'Where have all the flowers gone?' among the top 20 political songs. It was written by the late Pete Seeger in 1955, expanded by Joe Hickerson in 1960 and immortalized by Joan Baez in the 1960s as a protest song. After reflecting on the terrible loss of life in war, each verse ends with a line charged with a tone that is plaintive but also filled with inevitable acceptance, 'When will they ever learn? When will they ever learn?'

The same is true in all efforts – personal, intrapersonal, social, national, international and environmental – towards reconciliation. On the one hand, reconciliation is the goal towards which we work in response to an inner longing and aspiration. Using theological terminology, it is an eschatological goal. Though we accept that it cannot be reached in this life, it is possible to have reconciliation-shaped lives, working towards a reconciliation-filled society. On the other hand, it is possible to enjoy moments of reconciliation (small 'r') that can elicit great acts of generosity and heroism on the way to Reconciliation (big 'R').

At the same time we live as though our finger hovers over a self-destruct button, and it would not take too much to press it. Up until the 1990s there was the threat of nuclear annihilation. While this has receded (though not disappeared), other demons have come to taunt us, most specifically the way the planet is treated and the earth's resources are shared. The threats come from unexpected directions – such as water, which is going to be an issue of the future. Water covers 70 per cent of the earth's surface, though less than one per cent is drinkable. As the earth's population increases there will be an increasing call on this decreasing resource. Already there are water disputes between countries and communities – witness the long-standing disagreements between Israel and Palestine, where it is claimed that Israel controls the majority of Palestinian water. Any realistic agreement over the vexed issue of Palestinian autonomy will need to include agreement over water supply.

When will we ever learn? Enmity as well as reconciliation is hardwired into human nature and nothing will change that in this world. Just as human beings can rise to acts of stunning heroism, so too we can sink to depths of appalling atrocities. Just as, through our shared humanity, we can bask in the celebration of the former, so too, through that same shared humanity, we need to recognize some responsibility in the latter no matter how far away or remote.

But we can make a difference. Desmond Tutu often tells the story of how the direction his life took was deeply affected and encouraged by his seeing a white man – Fr Trevor Huddleston, priest in Sophiatown – raising his hat to greet the then young Desmond Tutu's mother. A white man making a respectful greeting to an African was unheard of in Apartheid-ridden South Africa. This simple gesture was a culturally radical action that made all the difference in the world to Desmond Tutu. The gesture was no off-the-cuff, out-of-character action, it was instinctive and spontaneous. It welled up from someone with a deep sense of justice and respect for humanity, seeing each person, regardless of ethnicity, as a child of God. It is people of commitment who can make a difference even through spontaneous actions.

Having emphasized the importance of the Church taking its relationship with culture more seriously, we now develop this further by looking at some cultural trends in British society.

Church and society

We have seen that society is involved in reconciliation. Often reconciliation is viewed primarily as conflict resolution – as the various truth and reconciliation commissions show – but there are also examples where it has gone further by digging deeper into remembering, pointing to transformation and involving celebration. It is also significant that on occasions – such as forgiveness farming – reconciliation is defined by using theological terms. The involvement of people of faith in reconciliation projects is also important. Our concentration has been on the Christian faith, but people of other faiths are of course frequently involved in peace and reconciliation activities.

While countries may seek reconciliation as a building-block in the reconstruction of society, it is central to Christian identity. Whenever Christians are involved in reconciliation they are creating a context where Jesus Christ, the embodiment of reconciliation, can be recognized. Reconciliation is mission. Indeed the Church is called to be a reconciling church in a reconciling world. It is an agent of reconciliation, and its role in relation to the world is not simply to engage with but to change it. At the same time the Church needs to be ready to be changed by the God already at work in the world, outside the institution of the Church – the Church is part of God's kingdom and needs to be alert to what God is saying, from within the Church and from within the world.

In order to be a reconciling church in a reconciling world, the Church works with bodies that are promoting reconciliation. As a relationship develops, the Church should be clear about the basis of the relationship. Partnership is the basis for many such relationships, all parties collaborating where possible and sharing the tasks and responsibilities – but there are limits to a relationship based purely on partnership. For while the language of partnership accurately indicates a desire for the Church to work alongside other people and agencies, it does so on the unspoken premise that all involved espouse the same values and working practices – partnership may articulate a way of God relating to the world but it falls short on relating the world to God. It may well be that the Church will find itself doing the work of an NGO if other agencies in the partnership withdraw. It is far better to move from the concept of partnership to that of mutuality in its relationships with other bodies. Mutuality recognizes shared interests and priorities of all involved but at the same time accepts difference and distinctiveness, so that other agencies can be true to their aims and objectives and the Church faithful to its calling in service to the community. This is not a blank cheque for proselytizing but a mechanism for respecting difference and otherness. It will ensure that reconciliation can be seen as much richer and wider than conflict resolution, important though that may be.

In Chapter 5 we argued the need for the Church to become more involved in culture, which has a significant role in defining a society's identity. This final part of the book reflects on some cultural trends in British society, with questions about the extent to which society provides an environment for fruitful engagement with reconciliation. It suggests ways the Church can help increase society's openness to reconciliation.

Society in the UK

The time when the Christian Church played a significant role in British society has long gone. Bishops in the House of Lords and presiding over coronations and royal weddings are vestiges of the past and there is no guarantee these will continue long into the future. There are places where the Church remains a vibrant part of the community even though the vicar is learning to exercise ministry in different ways and to share that ministry with others. However, there are also places where the Church is weak or absent. The number of weddings, baptisms and funerals taken by clergy has declined: many weddings no longer take place in church but at wedding venues, and an increasing number of funerals are being taken by secular and civil celebrants.

This massive change began when it looked as though society no longer needed God. Eventually we would become a secular society, it was being argued. A culture that was putting its faith in materialism had no place for God. However, it soon became clear that it was the Church as an institution in which people were losing faith. Many, in the words of the sociologist Grace Davie, wanted to believe but not belong.[7] People recognized churches as holy places and would go there for weddings, funerals and baptisms and perhaps for Christmas and Harvest Festival. But they did not want to join the people of God gathered there. Graham Ward succinctly summed up the climate with these words: 'Postmodernity's religion was not about discipline, sacrifice, obedience, and the development of virtue. It was more related to the spiritualizing of human subjectivity.'[8] Davie ends her landmark book *Religion in Britain Since 1945: Believing without Belonging* with a quote from an unpublished paper by the sociologist David Martin that captures the final decade of the twentieth century:

> We in England live in the chill religious vapours of northern Europe, where moribund religious establishments loom over populations that mostly do not enter churches of public worship even if they entertain inchoate beliefs. Yet these establishments guard and maintain thousands of houses of God, which are markers of space and time. Not only are they markers and anchors, but also the only repositories of all-embracing meanings pointing beyond the immediate to the ultimate. They are the only institutions that deal in tears and concern themselves with the breaking points of human existence. They provide frames and narratives and signs to live by, and offer persistent points of reference. They are repositories of signs about miraculous birth and redemptive sacrifice, shared tables and gift-giving; and they offer moral codes and exemplars for the creation of communal solidarity and the nourishment of virtue. They are

> places from which to launch initiatives which help sustain the kind of networks found, for example, in the inner city; they welcome schools and regiments and rotary clubs; they celebrate and commemorate; they are islands of quietness; they are places in which unique gestures occur of blessing, distribution and obeisance; they offer spaces in which solemnly to gather, to sing, to lay flowers and light candles. They are – in Philip Larkin's phrase – serious places on serious earth.[9]

Those who predicted the end of faith and belief have been proved wrong. The dreadful events that happened in the USA on September 11, 2001 have raised the prominence of faiths and religions on the world stage; and the UK, confronted by the London bombings on 7 July, 2005, had a similar reminder.

There was another cultural movement that found materialism and secularism lacking. People wanted to believe there was more to the world than could be perceived by the five senses. There was a renewed search for transcendence, something beyond the world in which we lived. Transcendence and otherness are close relatives. Ward describes this as a period of 'post-secularity' when religion was becoming visible again.[10] It was an age of 're-enchantment' for the modern world. The Christian faith had receded to the edges of society and was not engaging with culture in any vigorous way, and yet questions about the purpose and meaning of life and what happens after death would not go away. They may be questions that were discussed in churches but they were not discussed in the public square, and so they emerged in different ways.

Three epic 'Lord of the Rings' films include such themes as the battle between good and evil and raise the possibility of immortality, an issue to which we shall be returning below. The Harry Potter books, with much of their action in another world, became bestsellers to say the least – and significantly, English cathedrals provided the sets for some of the resulting films. The *Da Vinci Code*, with its overt religious theme, was popular as a book and film. Angels, demons, ghosts and vampires are regular visitors to our TV screens. Hallowe'en has become increasingly popular and more frequently observed. There has been increased interest in alternative spiritualities and new religious movements such as Pagan pathways. Ward comments: 'Religion has become a special effect, inseparably bound to an entertainment value.'[11] Christian faith and belief are viewed differently. In a society where choice is given a high priority, faith is regarded as one activity among the many for which people can opt.

It is with cultural trends such as these that the gospel needs to engage. These are the rivers that feed society's social and political agendas. If the Church wishes to make a real difference to society, it is at this level that it needs to work. By the time it reaches Parliament, the question is almost certainly decided, as we have seen with the Equal Marriage Act. Some would argue that the Church's influence at any level of society is minimal. There is no way to prove this either way, but as will emerge below there is anecdotal evidence that it may have more influence than some think. The kingdom is larger than the Church and there are many people, Christians and non-Christians, espousing kingdom values who would be able to influence culture – the number of reconciliation activities in society and the number of Christians involved testify to that. We now consider some ways the Church can respond to contemporary cultural trends and highlight the significance of the reconciliation agenda for them.

The Church's response

The significance of death

The first response is in an area in which the Church is already involved, and one that has a profound effect on society and its approach to reconciliation, namely death. Society has banished death to the outer recesses of human living and, paradoxically, elements of life with it. Society manages death but would rather not face it. Death started its journey away from its former prominent place in society in the wake of the industrial revolution, when there was no space in overcrowded cities to bury the dead. Cemeteries were built on the outskirts of cities; there were even trains to take the dead way out into the rural areas for their final resting places.[12]

However, there was a visible shift in society's attitude towards and handling of death in the period after the Second World War. With the phenomenal advance of medicine and cures for so many diseases came the implicit belief that death itself was in jeopardy. This aspiration had been around for centuries but was now looking possible. People became more fixed on the message of medicine (regarded as purveyor of life) and less on that of the Church and clergy (regarded as purveyors of death). One of the outcomes was that medicine took over end-of-life care, leading to the 'medicalization of death'. Whereas in the past a family recognized when death was coming, was prepared for it and ensured that the dying person was also prepared, now those approaching death were being taken to hospitals, whose primary objective was to make people better. Hospitals were not really prepared for death. Fortunately, today, the hospice movement provides environments where the reality of death is faced in all its mystery and fear, but the prevailing attitude remains. Although faith communities take death and the ceremonies surrounding it very seriously, society generally is unwilling to face it.

Indeed society has forgotten the art of dying. In the past the mystery of death and dying was acknowledged and managed by employing rituals: the family would be gathered; the priest would say prayers; nearest relatives would wear black. In some places the clocks would be stopped and, following the traditional English custom that even spread to parts of Europe and New England, the bees would be told.[13] Such rituals gave permission for people to act unusually – sometimes incomprehensibly – in the face of the incomprehensible. But in an increasingly fragmenting society, where faith and symbolism are being sidelined and not being in control is considered a flaw in humanity, we are losing touch with rituals that are a support in the face of death. The logical consequence of this is that death is regarded as an ordinary, everyday occurrence rather than as the mystery that it is because society has lost faith in the language and action with which it needs to be negotiated and managed. Businesses like the Swiss company Dignitas, which are embodiments of assisted suicide, are the logical outcome. They mistakenly believe that they provide places where control is clawed back and mystery is removed.[14]

Contemporary society's embarrassment with death impinges on a number of the cultural trends already identified. The spiritual vacuum that accompanied materialism and secularism cannot cope with death because it cannot satisfactorily explain or manage it. The reality of death challenges the assertion that this world is the totality of life and existence. The 're-enchantment' of the world that Ward describes opens doors to a new relationship.

As already indicated, the reality of death is a clear statement that there is a limit to the control human beings have over their lives and the environment. Humanity has limitations. This is a harsh message in an age when it appears that everything can be controlled from somewhere. It is possible to control drones that wreak death and destruction in one part of the world from the safety of another. It is possible to relay news from one part of the world to another, informing of events seconds after they happen. The computer game *Second Life* even enables players to have total control over life by 'living' in a virtual world, taking on an identity of their choosing, marrying and having children. But the reality of death puts perspective into all these possibilities and raises questions about their value. It is not surprising that for centuries a 'cure' for death has been sought and that society, having failed to find one, is taking the route of devaluing it or pretending it does not exist.

The Christian faith faces the reality of death and then transforms it through the death and resurrection of Jesus Christ. The importance of this for Christianity and for reconciliation is that while the reality of death and the pain surrounding it have to be taken seriously, it is not the end. The resurrection of Christ has transformed death from an impenetrable wall to a gateway to something new and fresh. Death, then, was a sign of enmity between God and humanity until Christ transformed it into an opportunity for reconciliation. His death on the cross was the moment God was reconciled to humanity.

St Paul devoted the longest chapter of his two letters to the Christians in Corinth (1 Cor. 15) to death and resurrection – having a clear understanding was important for him. Death and resurrection does not just refer to what happens at the end of life but to every ending and new beginning throughout life.

The question of death has been discussed at some length because it touches on a number of the other cultural issues with which the Church can engage. Churches are already involved pastorally through conducting funerals. But as well as supporting the bereaved, it is also important for congregations to discuss their understandings of death and how to prepare for it. Also important is its significance within society as a whole. How does our understanding of death affect our values and the way life is lived? How is it possible to get this higher up on society's agenda? One way of highlighting the importance of this topic within churches is for each member of each congregation – regardless of age – to write their funeral service.

Telling the story

The second response concerns story – we have already considered its importance in reconciliation and the Christian faith. The Church needs to take every opportunity to tell the Christian story in ways that are creative, engaging and that speak into the heart of the questions society is asking. An increasing number of people do not know the Christian story. At the moment many are turning to Harry Potter and a host of vampires and ghosts to search for answers to questions materialism cannot answer. Vincent Donovan found ways of telling the Christian story with the Masai (see Chapter 4), so it can be done by Christians today. Donovan went out of the traditional mission stations and met with the Masai in places where they were most open to speaking. He first needed to listen to their stories and show that he was genuinely interested in them as God's children. He was able to address their questions and move them on to help them encounter Jesus Christ in ways that were culturally appropriate for them. It is important that Christians are aware of the questions non-church-attending society is asking, which will be different from those the Church is asking. Desmond Tutu once commented that Christians are very good at answering questions nobody else is asking.

One great resource that churches have is their schools. Approximately one million children and young people attend Church of England schools alone. Young people are cultural barometers and it is possible to learn a great deal from them about cultural trends. Already those attending church schools are learning the Christian story and its implications for daily life. They will also be discussing the stories at home with their parents. How do Christians ensure young people see a reality and authenticity in the stories of the Christian tradition? It is to this that we now turn in the next response. Storytelling is very important in all cultures. Enabling the Christian story to mix with others prepares fruitful ground for reconciliation.

Giving authenticity to the story

The third response concerns the role of the Church, which is crucial. The Church needs to witness to the values it espouses, which will give body and authenticity to faith. To paraphrase the words and sentiments of Graham Ward: it will need women and men committed to Jesus Christ whose commitment reflects such characteristics as discipline, sacrifice, obedience and the development of virtue. Chapter 5 looked at this through the lens of a reconciling church, and we saw that one of the marks of a reconciling church is the formation of reconciling communities such as the Kenward Trust. In addition there are religious communities across the world that embody the values of an authentic witnessing church. There is the ecumenical community of Taizé in France, a parable of reconciliation that continues to attract young people from across the world in their thousands. Reconciliation is at the heart of Taizé's rule of life, amplified by the community's church being called the Church of Reconciliation.[15] Sant'Egidio in Rome is a movement of lay people dedicated to evangelization and solidarity with the poor – it has more than 60,000 adherents spread across 73 countries and places emphasis on reconciliation.

Church and kingdom

Finally, the number of Christians in the world involved in all kinds of movements towards reconciliation is countless. This book has given examples of reconciliation projects, groups and organizations as well as truth and reconciliation commissions. Another reason for ensuring that the Church is true to its calling is the importance of resourcing and sending out into the world women and men devoted to Christ who will continue the work of reconciliation in countless ways. This is the work of the kingdom of God.

A reconciling life, a reconciling church and a reconciling society are interrelated. Christians should be at home in all three places and able to move effortlessly between them. Like Nelson Mandela's speech from the dock during his trial for treason in 1964 with which this book began, the vision of reconciliation may not be established in this life but it does provide a shape and purpose for it. True reconciliation is a journey of a lifetime.

For individual, quiet reflection

1 Listen to some music that you find brings inner reconciliation.
2 Reflect on your funeral service.
3 How does your local church witness to the values it espouses? How do you do the same?

For discussion in groups

1 Is reconciliation both a longing and aspiration for people of faith and also a cry at the heart of the whole of creation?
2 If freedom can be born in song, which songs do you know, secular or religious, that might be liberating for you as individuals – or for Church or society – or that might help towards reconciliation where there is suspicion or conflict?
3 'Important cause' or 'expendable luxury': what is your assessment of humankind's concern for the environment, and are there specific issues that individuals as well as governments need to address to achieve harmony and reconciliation within creation?
4 Discuss your funeral services.
5 Is your church creative in the ways it tells the Christian story? How could it be more so?

Prayer

God of the ages, whose Spirit at creation moved in the darkness upon the face of the waters, bringing harmony and light, and who made humankind in your own image that is the pattern of love, peace and wholeness:

Grant us the resilience to struggle to defeat evil and never to placate it;
to seek renewal and reconciliation;
and to work for that time when nations will take history in their hands and bend the arc of the moral universe towards justice.

This we ask in the name of him who on the cross reconciled humankind to the God of the ages, and whose Spirit at creation moved in the darkness upon the face of the waters, bringing harmony and light, your son Jesus Christ, our Lord. Amen.

(Based on tributes to Nelson Mandela by President Barack Obama and Archbishop Justin Welby)

Derek Carpenter

Appendix
Reconciliation liturgies

1 Reconciliation and the Christian tradition

Greeting

Grace, mercy and peace from God our Father and the Lord Jesus Christ be with you.
And also with you.

Bible reading and act of thanksgiving

So if anyone is in Christ, there is a new creation: everything old has passed away; see, everything has become new! All this is from God, who reconciled us to himself through Christ, and has given us the ministry of reconciliation; that is, in Christ God was reconciling the world to himself, not counting their trespasses against them, and entrusting the message of reconciliation to us. (2 Cor. 5.17–19)

A brief time for silence, reflection and thanksgiving. In the period of thanksgiving, give thanks to God for acts of reconciliation you have witnessed and experienced over the last week. You may wish to share these with others in the group.

A prayer of penitence

Father, we confess that so often, when those of different races have been oppressed by their history,
  pride has triumphed over humility;
  disobedience has defeated your will for humankind;
  self-interest has held sway over generosity of spirit;
  and that blindness has overcome the vision you have set before us

of a harmony to be restored,
a kingdom to be sought,
and a world to be reconciled
in your Son who has reconciled all people to you through his Cross,
even Jesus Christ our Lord.

Derek Carpenter

A symbolic act

Each in turn light a small tea light, and place it at the foot of a cross in the centre of the group.

Closing prayer

May God sustain us on our journey, give us those gifts needful for our pilgrimage, and travel with us along the road, until we meet him face to face. **Amen.**

2 Drivers of reconciliation

Greeting

The grace of our Lord Jesus Christ, the love of God, and the fellowship of the Holy Spirit be with you all.
And also with you.

Bible reading and act of thanksgiving

How very good and pleasant it is when kindred live together in unity! It is like the precious oil on the head, running down upon the beard, on the beard of Aaron, running down over the collar of his robes. It is like the dew of Hermon, which falls on the mountains of Zion. For the LORD ordained his blessing, life for evermore. (Ps. 133)

A brief time for silence, reflection and thanksgiving. In the period of thanksgiving, give thanks to God for acts of reconciliation you have witnessed and experienced over the last week. You may wish to share these with others in the group.

A prayer of penitence

Almighty God, Spirit of purity and grace, in asking thy forgiveness I cannot claim a right to be forgiven but only cast myself upon thine unbounded love.

I can plead no merit or desert:
I can plead no extenuating circumstances:
I cannot plead the frailty of my nature:
I cannot plead the force of the temptations I encounter:
I cannot plead the persuasions of others who led me astray:
I can only say, for the sake of Jesus Christ thy Son, my Lord. Amen.

John Baillie, 1886–1960

A symbolic act

Offer each other a sign of peace, with an accompanying encouraging word.

Closing prayer

Glory be to you, God, who created us:
Glory be to you, Jesus, who redeemed us:
Glory be to you, Holy Spirit, who gives us new life:
Glory be to God, Father, Son and Holy Spirit, now and for evermore. Amen.

3 Marks of reconciliation

Greeting

In the name of the Father, and of the Son, and of the Holy Spirit.
Amen.
The Lord be with you.
And also with you.

Bible reading and act of thanksgiving

He is the image of the invisible God, the firstborn of all creation; for in him all things in heaven and on earth were created, things visible and invisible, whether thrones or dominions or rulers or powers – all things have been created through him and for him. For in him all the fullness of God was pleased to dwell, and through him God was pleased to reconcile to himself all things, whether on earth or in heaven, by making peace through the blood of his cross. (Col. 1.15–16, 19–20)

A brief time for silence, reflection and thanksgiving. In the period of thanksgiving, give thanks to God for acts of reconciliation you have witnessed and experienced over the last week. You may wish to share these with others in the group.

A prayer of penitence

Father, forgive us
  that when you have spoken your call has met with a feeble response or we have failed to listen;
  that we have been unwilling to overcome the differences that divide;
  that the vision you have set before us has been blurred by self-interest;
  that we have missed opportunities to recognize elements of truth and justice in faiths other than our own;
  that we have failed to disturb complacency and to respect the dignity of others;
  and that we have so often been defeated by the barriers of race, culture and language.
Father, forgive.

Derek Carpenter

A symbolic act

Into a bowl of water, each in turn drop a small pebble and wait until the surface is again calm. See the pebble as your sins sunk to the bottom of the ocean of God's love, and the ripples as his love extending to you and, beyond you, to the whole of creation.

Closing prayer

May God, who in Christ gives us a spring of water welling up to eternal life, perfect in us the image of his glory; and may his blessing be with us all, now and always. **Amen.**

4 A reconciling life

Greeting

We stand alongside each other in our brokenness, inviting God's healing for us and for his world.
You are the God of wholeness: grant us your presence and your peace.

Bible reading and act of thanksgiving

But I say to you that if you are angry with a brother or sister, you will be liable to judgement; and if you insult a brother or sister, you will be liable to the council; and if you say, 'You fool', you will be liable to the hell of fire. So when you are offering your gift at the altar, if you remember that your brother or sister has something against you, leave your gift there before the altar and go; first be reconciled to your brother or sister, and then come and offer your gift. (Matt. 5.22–24)

A brief time for silence, reflection and thanksgiving. In the period of thanksgiving, give thanks to God for acts of reconciliation you have witnessed and experienced over the last week. You may wish to share these with others in the group.

A prayer of penitence

Build us up, O Father, into the fellowship of the free that starts in each family and reaches out to the people next door, that starts in our own congregation and reaches over barriers of custom and prejudice to the church down the street, that starts in our own country and reaches beyond patriotism and national pride to the nations of the world, that starts with our own colour and rejoices to claim as brothers and sisters people of every race. Lead us all, O wide and loving Father, to the Kingdom of your dear Son, where there is no pain and no fear, no hunger and no greed, no oppressor and no oppressed, but all are full-grown people in Christ, our only Lord and Saviour.

John Kingsnorth (adapted)

A symbolic act

Spend two or three minutes writing privately on a small piece of paper what is most on your heart for which you wish to seek forgiveness. The leader then offers this prayer:

God, cleanse me from my sins, and make a new heart within me.

Then move outside and burn the paper in the assurance of forgiveness.

Closing prayer

May the Lord Jesus be near us to watch over us,
Within us to give us his strength,
Behind us to shield us from all harm,
Before us to guide us along right pathways,
and above us to bless us now and at all times. **Amen.**

5 A reconciling church

Greeting

God, Creator, Redeemer, Sanctifier: you are with us always and everywhere.

Give us the assurance of your presence, now and at all times.

Bible reading and act of thanksgiving

Let me hear what God the LORD will speak, for he will speak peace to his people, to his faithful, to those who turn to him in their hearts. Surely his salvation is at hand for those who fear him, that his glory may dwell in our land. Steadfast love and faithfulness will meet; righteousness and peace will kiss each other. Faithfulness will spring up from the ground, and righteousness will look down from the sky. The LORD will give what is good, and our land will yield its increase. Righteousness will go before him and will make a path for his steps. (Ps. 85.8–13)

A brief time for silence, reflection and thanksgiving. In the period of thanksgiving, give thanks to God for acts of reconciliation you have witnessed and experienced over the last week. You may wish to share these with others in the group.

A prayer of penitence

Father forgive them for they know not what they do.
Father forgive us for we know what we do.

Derek Carpenter

A symbolic act

Each member of the group holds a length of ribbon (about 30 cm long). One by one, tie your ribbon to that of the person next to you – the last person in the group completes the circle. All hold together the completed circle as a sign of your unity in Christ, and say together:
Let us together pursue all that makes for peace and builds up the body of Christ.

Closing prayer

May God grant us grace to be at peace among ourselves, to be joyful and to pray with a thankful heart. May he make us holy in every way, and keep our whole being – spirit, soul and body – free from every fault at the coming of the Lord Jesus. And may we keep faith with him as he keeps faith with us. **Amen.** (based on 1 Thess. 5)

6 A reconciling society

Greeting

God, in whom we live and move and have our being
You made us for yourself, so that our hearts are restless till they rest in you:
Grant that in your light we may see light
and that in your service we might find perfect freedom.

Bible reading and act of thanksgiving

For if while we were enemies, we were reconciled to God through the death of his Son, much more surely, having been reconciled, will we be saved by his life. But more than that, we even boast in God through our Lord Jesus Christ, through whom we have now received reconciliation. (Rom. 5.10–11)

A brief time for silence, reflection and thanksgiving. In the period of thanksgiving, give thanks to God for acts of reconciliation you have witnessed and experienced over the last week. You may wish to share these with others in the group.

A prayer of penitence

O God our Father, help us to nail to the cross of thy dear Son the whole body of our death, the wrong desires of the heart, the sinful devisings of the mind, the corrupt apprehensions of the eyes, the cruel words of the tongue, the ill employment of hands and feet; that the old self being crucified and done away, the new self may live and grow into the glorious likeness of the same thy Son Jesus Christ, who liveth and reigneth with thee and the Holy Ghost, one God, world without end.

Eric Milner-White, 1884–1964 (adapted)

A symbolic act

Sitting in a circle with a crucifix in the centre, slowly rotate it so that each is looking, for a while, on the image of the crucified Christ.

Closing prayer

May the setting sun be God's assurance that sins have been forgiven, and the sun's rising give birth to a new day of resurrection hope and new life in Jesus Christ our Lord. **Amen.**

For general use

Litany of reconciliation from Coventry Cathedral

All have sinned and fallen short of the glory of God.
The hatred which divides nation from nation, race from race, class from class
Father, forgive.

The covetous desires of people and nations to possess what is not their own
Father, forgive.

The greed which exploits the work of human hands and lays waste the earth
Father, forgive.

Our envy of the welfare and happiness of others
Father, forgive.

Our indifference to the plight of the imprisoned, the homeless, the refugee
Father, forgive.

The lust which dishonours the bodies of men, women and children
Father, forgive.

The pride which leads us to trust in ourselves and not in God
Father, forgive.

Be kind to one another, tender-hearted, forgiving one another, as God in Christ forgave you.

Copyright acknowledgements

Every effort has been made to seek permission to use copyright material reproduced in this book. The publisher apologizes for those cases where permission might not have been sought and, if notified, will formally seek permission at the earliest opportunity. The publisher and author acknowledge with thanks permission to reproduce extracts from the following.

Extracts from *Common Worship: Services and Prayers* are copyright © The Archbishops' Council, 2000, and are reproduced by permission. All rights reserved. <copyright@churchofengland.org>

Liturgies and prayers are by Derek Carpenter unless otherwise stated. Reproduced by permission.

The prayer by John Kingsnorth is reproduced by permission.

The prayer by Eric Milner-White is reproduced by permission of SPCK.

The prayer by John Baillie is reproduced by permission of Oxford University Press.

The Coventry Cathedral Litany of Reconciliation is reproduced by permission of the Dean.

Notes

Introduction

1 Nelson Mandela, *Long Walk to Freedom: The Autobiography of Nelson Mandela*, London, Little, Brown, 1994, p. 354.
2 Mandela, *Long Walk to Freedom*, p. 617.
3 The five marks of mission are now:
'To proclaim the Good News of the Kingdom;
To teach, baptise and nurture new believers;
To respond to human need by loving service;
To seek to transform unjust structures of society, to challenge violence of every kind and to pursue peace and reconciliation;
To strive to safeguard the integrity of creation and sustain and renew the life of the earth' – <www.anglicancommunion.org/ministry/mission/fivemarks.cfm>.

1 Reconciliation and the Christian tradition

1 While the majority of New Testament scholars recognize that reconciliation is a theme in Paul's thinking and writing, they are not unanimous on its significance for his theology. Some argue that it is not too important, others that it is at the heart of his understanding of God and Jesus Christ. I am persuaded by the latter group.
2 See Corneliu Constantineanu, *The Social Significance of Reconciliation in Paul's Theology: Narrative Readings in Romans*, London and New York, T. & T. Clark, 2010. I am grateful for a number of insights provided by this book.
3 A term used by the Archbishop of Canterbury, Justin Welby.
4 John Chryssavis, *In the Heart of the Desert: The Spirituality of the Desert Fathers and Mothers*, Bloomington, IN, World Wisdom Inc., 2008, pp. 15ff.
5 Benedicta Ward, *The Sayings of the Desert Fathers: The Alphabetical Collection*, Kalamazoo, MI, Cistercian Publications, 1975, p. 3.

6 Ward, *Sayings of the Desert Fathers*, p. 6.
7 Sam Wells, 'The Exasperating Patience of God', unpublished lecture, Faith in Conflict Conference, Coventry Cathedral, 26 February 2013.

2 Drivers of reconciliation

1 Ben Maclellan, *A Proper Degree of Terror: John Graham and the Cape's Eastern Frontier*, Johannesburg, Ravan Press, 1986.
2 Stanley Hauerwas, 'Why Time Cannot and Should Not Heal the Wounds of History but Time Has Been and Can Be Redeemed', *Scottish Journal of Theology* 53:1 (2000), p. 35.
3 Commission on Theological Concerns of the Christian Conference of Asia (ed.), *Minjung Theology: People as the Subjects of History*, New York, Orbis, 1981.
4 For a fuller exploration, see Brian Castle, *Reconciling One and All: God's Gift to the World*, London, SPCK, 2008, pp. 32ff.
5 Nelson Mandela, *Long Walk to Freedom*, London, Little, Brown, 1994, pp. 516ff.
6 Fanny Crosby: America's Hymn Queen: <www.christianity.com/church/church-history/timeline/1801-1900/fanny-crosby-americas-hymn-queen-11630385.html>.
7 Hannah Arendt, *The Human Condition*, Chicago, University of Chicago Press, [1958] 1998, pp. 238–9.
8 Ian Bradley, 'The Sound of Forgiveness', *The Times*, 5 January 2013, <www.thetimes.co.uk/tto/faith/article3648357.ece>.

3 Marks of reconciliation

1 Brian Castle, *Reconciling One and All: God's Gift to the World*, London, SPCK, 2008.
2 See Timothy Radcliffe, *Take the Plunge: Living Baptism and Confirmation*, London, Bloomsbury, 2012, p. 172.
3 Rowan Williams, *Silence and Honey Cakes: The Wisdom of the Desert*, Oxford, Lion, 2003, p. 49.
4 'Why are Men so Angry that they Kill Children to Get What they Want?', Joanna Moorhead, *The Guardian*, 3 August 2013.
5 Stephen Grosz, *The Examined Life: How We Lose and Find Ourselves*, London, Vintage Books, 2013, p. 9.
6 Grosz, *Examined Life*, p. 10.

7 The Eucharist is also known as Holy Communion and the Lord's Supper.

8 Colin Patterson and Alastair McKay, *Making Mediation Work – In the Church of England*, London, Bridge Builders Ministries, 2012, p. 7.

9 Quoted in Michael Marshall, *Church at the Crossroads: Lambeth 1988*, London, Collins, 1988, p. xi.

10 I am grateful to the Revd Harvey Richardson, a musician and theologian, for drawing my attention to Schönberg's term.

11 A very good summary of Schönberg's concept can be found at 'Emancipation of the dissonance', <http://en.wikipedia.org/wiki/Emancipation_of_the_dissonance>.

12 Quoted in Timothy Radcliffe, *What is the Point of Being a Christian?* London, Burns & Oates, 2005, p. 187.

4 A reconciling life

1 Joel Salatin, 'Forgiveness Farming', *Acres USA: The Voice of Eco-Agriculture* 37:12 (December 2006).

2 Barbara Ehrenreich, *Dancing in the Streets: A History of Collective Joy*, London: Granta, 2007.

3 Ehrenreich, *Dancing in the Streets*, pp. 57ff.

4 Ehrenreich, *Dancing in the Streets*, pp. 62–4.

5 See Eamon Duffy's fascinating account of the Reformation as viewed from the ordinary people in *The Voices of Morebath: Reformation and Rebellion in an English Village*, New Haven and London, Yale University Press, 2003.

6 Michael Argyle, *The Social Psychology of Leisure*, London, Penguin, 1996.

7 Ehrenreich, *Dancing in the Streets*, p. 152.

8 *Common Worship: Services of the Church of England*, Eucharistic Prayers for use in Order One, Prayer F, London, Church House Publishing, 2000, p. 198.

9 Brian Castle, 'Justice is What the UK Needs, Not Fairness', *Church Times*, 24 February, 2012.

10 *Common Worship*, An Order for Morning Prayer on Sunday, p. 32.

11 Vincent Donovan, *Christianity Rediscovered*, London, SCM Press, 1982.

12 Benedicta Ward, *The Sayings of the Desert Fathers: The Alphabetical Collection*, Kalamazoo, MI, Cistercian Publications, 1975, p. 229.
13 Stephen Grosz, *The Examined Life: How We Lose and Find Ourselves*, London, Vintage Books, 2013, pp. 18ff.

5 A reconciling church

1 See Brian Castle, *Unofficial God? Voices from Beyond the Walls*, London, SPCK, 2004, pp. 130–45.
2 For a fuller exposition of this analysis, see Walter Hollenweger, 'Intercultural Theology', *Theological Renewal* 10 (October 1978), pp. 2–14.
3 In 2 Cor. 5.16—7.2 there are a number of clear indications that Paul views the Corinthian response as a rejection of him.
4 See Geoffrey Burn, 'Land and Reconciliation in Australia: A Theological Approach', University of Exeter, PhD thesis, 2010, pp. 77ff.
5 Clifford Geertz, *The Interpretation of Cultures*, London, Fontana, 1993, p. 5, quoted in Timothy Gorringe, *Furthering Humanity: A Theology of Culture*, Aldershot, Ashgate, 2004, p. 3.
6 Gorringe, *Furthering Humanity*, p. 3.
7 Hadani Ditmars, *Dancing in the No-Fly Zone: A Woman's Journey Through Iraq*, Northampton, MA, Olive Branch Press, 2006, pp. 57ff. and 163ff.
8 Rock and pop cultures are essential aids in understanding the spiritual struggles of adolescence – see Castle, *Unofficial God? Voices from Beyond the Walls*, pp. 111–16.
9 The term 'mass culture' was commonly used in the 1930s and is related to the totalitarianism of that period. Some regarded it as a synthetic culture that threatened the freedom of the personality by the pressure of economic forces – see Gorringe, *Furthering Humanity*, p. 53.
10 N. Postman, *Amusing Ourselves to Death*, London, Methuen, 1986, quoted in Gorringe, *Furthering Humanity*, p. 56.
11 BBC Radio 4, *Start the Week*, Monday 11 November, 2013.
12 Faith and Order Commission of the Church of England, *Men and Women in Marriage*, GS Misc. 1046, London, Church House

Publishing, 2013, section 17; also available at <www.churchofengland.org/media/1715479/marriagetextbrochureprint.pdf>.

13 See Faith and Order Commission, *Men and Women in Marriage*, section 22.

14 The House of Bishops of the Church of England issued the following guidance on same-sex marriage: <www.churchofengland.org/media-centre/news/2014/02/house-of-bishops-pastoral-guidance-on-same-sex-marriage.aspx>.

15 The *Report of the House of Bishops Working Group on Human Sexuality* (The Pilling Report, GS Misc 1929), London, Church House Publishing, 2013.

16 See Church of England, Statement from the College of Bishops, 27 January 2014 – <www.churchofengland.org/media-centre/news/2014/01/statement-from-the-college-of-bishops.aspx>.

17 Some of this is drawn from my article published in the *Church Times*, 'Listening, Consensus, Worship . . . If that Doesn't Sound Like Synodical Government, Why Not?' 16 April, 2010 – see also under Publications on www.briancastle.org.

18 Anglican–Roman Catholic International Commission (ARCIC), *The Gift of Authority*, London, Catholic Truth Society, 1999.

19 <http://continuingindaba.com/about-2/>.

20 The incident referred to is the killing of Lee Rigby on 22 May, 2013.

21 Taken from brochure, *Ecumenical Institute at Château de Bossey*.

22 *Report of the House of Bishops Working Group on Human Sexuality*, which has a minority report within it, shows the breadth of interpretation and understanding within the Church of England.

23 <http://kenwardtrust.org.uk>.

24 In November 2012 the Supreme Court in Harare determined that Anglicans in the Church of the Province of Central Africa should be allowed back in their churches and that all properties taken from them – including schools and an orphanage – should be returned.

6 A reconciling society

1 See Brian Castle, *Reconciling One and All: God's Gift to the World*, London, SPCK, 2008, p. 1.

2 For the story of the Melanesian Brotherhood's work towards reconciliation and sacrifice in this dispute, see Castle, *Reconciling One and All*, pp. 22–3.

3 See <http://thejimmymizenfoundation.tumblr.com/> and <http://robknox.co.uk/>.

4 Joel Salatin, 'Forgiveness Farming', *Acres USA: The Voice of Eco-Agriculture* 37:12 (December 2006), pp. 16–21.

5 See: <www.newscientist.com/article/dn23060-has-global-warming-ground-to-a-halt.html#.Uqq_DdJdV2B>.

6 Jean Vanier, *Essential Writings*, selected and introduced by Carolyn Whitney-Brown, Modern Spiritual Masters Series, Maryknoll, NY, Orbis Books, 2008, p. 87.

7 Grace Davie, *Religion in Britain Since 1945: Believing without Belonging*, Oxford, Blackwell, 1994.

8 See Graham Ward, *The Politics of Discipleship: Becoming Postmaterial Citizens*, London, SCM Press, 2009, p. 157. I am grateful for Graham Ward's analysis, on which I have drawn in this section.

9 Davie, *Religion in Britain Since 1945*, pp. 189–90.

10 Ward, *Politics of Discipleship*, p. 117.

11 Ward, *Politics of Discipleship*, p. 149.

12 The London Necropolis Company established Brookwood Cemetery in Woking, Surrey, in 1848. Bodies came by train from London Necropolis Station, near Waterloo, and went to one of two stations at the Brookwood Cemetery: the south for the deceased of the Church of England and the north for deceased Roman Catholics and Non-Conformists.

13 John Greenleaf Whittier, source of the hymn, 'Dear Lord and Father of Mankind', wrote a poem, 'Telling the Bees'.

14 Some of this is drawn from my article published in the *Church Times*, 'Resources for Learning to Die', 1 July, 2011 – see also under Publications on <www.briancastle.org/>.

15 I discuss Taizé in some detail in *Reconciling One and All*, p. 101.

Bibliography

Anglican–Roman Catholic International Commission (ARCIC), *The Gift of Authority*, London, Catholic Truth Society, 1999.

Arendt, Hannah, *The Human Condition*, Chicago, University of Chicago Press, [1958] 1998.

Argyle, Michael, *The Social Psychology of Leisure*, London, Penguin, 1996.

Burn, Geoffrey, 'Reconciliation and Land in Australia', *Pacifica: Australasian Theological Studies* 24:1 (2011), pp. 80–100.

Castle, Brian, *Unofficial God? Voices from Beyond the Walls*, London, SPCK, 2004.

Castle, Brian, *Reconciling One and All: God's Gift to the World*, London, SPCK, 2008.

Chryssavis, John, *In the Heart of the Desert: The Spirituality of the Desert Fathers and Mothers*, Bloomington, IN, World Wisdom Inc., 2008.

Commission on Theological Concerns of the Christian Conference of Asia (CTC–CCA) (ed.), *Minjung Theology: People as the Subjects of History*, New York, Orbis, 1981.

Constantineanu, Corneliu, *The Social Significance of Reconciliation in Paul's Theology: Narrative Readings in Romans*, London and New York, T. & T. Clark, 2010.

Davie, Grace, *Religion in Britain Since 1945: Believing without Belonging*, Oxford, Blackwell, 1994.

Ditmars, Hadani, *Dancing in the No-Fly Zone: A Woman's Journey Through Iraq*, Northampton, MA, Olive Branch Press, 2006.

Donovan, Vincent, *Christianity Rediscovered*, London, SCM Press, 1982.

Duffy, Eamon, *The Voices of Morebath: Reformation and Rebellion in an English Village*, New Haven and London, Yale University Press, 2003.

Ehrenreich, Barbara, *Dancing in the Streets: A History of Collective Joy*, London, Granta Books, 2007.

Faith and Order Commission of the Church of England, *Men and Women in Marriage* (GS Misc. 1046), London, Church House Publishing, 2013.

Gorringe, Timothy, *Furthering Humanity: A Theology of Culture*, Aldershot, Ashgate, 2004.

Grosz, Stephen, *The Examined Life: How We Lose and Find Ourselves*, London, Vintage Books, 2013.

Hardage, Jeanette, *Mary Slessor – Everybody's Mother: The Era and Impact of a Victorian Missionary*, Eugene, OR, Wipf & Stock, 2008.

Hauerwas, Stanley, 'Why Time Cannot and Should Not Heal the Wounds of History but Time Has Been and Can Be Redeemed', *Scottish Journal of Theology* 53:1 (2000), pp. 33–49.

Hollenweger, Walter, 'Intercultural Theology', *Theological Renewal* 10 (October 1978), pp. 2–14.

Litten, Julian, *The English Way of Death*, London, Robert Hale, [1991] 1992.

Mandela, Nelson, *Long Walk to Freedom: The Autobiography of Nelson Mandela*, London, Little, Brown, 1994.

Marshall, Michael, *Church at the Crossroads: Lambeth 1988*, London, Collins, 1988.

Patterson, Colin and McKay, Alastair, *Making Mediation Work – In the Church of England*, Bridge Builders Ministries, 2012.

Radcliffe, Timothy, *Take the Plunge: Living Baptism and Confirmation*, London, Bloomsbury, 2012.

Radcliffe, Timothy, *What is the Point of Being a Christian?* London, Burns & Oates, 2005.

Salatin, Joel, 'Forgiveness Farming', *Acres USA: The Voice of Eco-Agriculture* 37:12 (December 2006), pp. 16–21.

Vanier, Jean, *Essential Writings*, selected and introduced by Carolyn Whitney-Brown, Modern Spiritual Masters Series, Maryknoll, NY, Orbis Books, 2008.

Verhey, Allen, *The Christian Art of Dying: Learning from Jesus*, Grand Rapids and Cambridge, Eerdmans, 2011.

Ward, Benedicta, *The Sayings of the Desert Fathers: The Alphabetical Collection*, London, Mowbrays, 1975.

Ward, Graham, *The Politics of Discipleship: Becoming Postmaterial Citizens*, London, SCM Press, 2009.

Williams, Rowan, *Silence and Honey Cakes: The Wisdom of the Desert*, Oxford, Lion, 2003.

Williams, Rowan, *Teresa of Avila*, London, Geoffrey Chapman, 1991.